STAND STRONG
FOR BOYS

90 FAITH-BUILDING DEVOTIONS

Our Daily Bread
Publishing™

Stand Strong for Boys: 90 Faith-Building Devotions
© 2021 by Our Daily Bread Ministries

ISBN: 978-1-64070-104-5

Printed in the United States of America
21 22 23 24 25 26 27 28 / 8 7 6 5 4 3 2 1

INTRODUCTION

Sometimes it is fun to find boyhood pictures of your favorite athletes—to see what they looked like when they were little. For instance, you can go online and find a picture of former Heisman Trophy winner Tim Tebow as a baby with his left hand touching a football. What a difference from the strong, muscular, football star of his adult years!

But the truth is, we all start that way. Small. Holding on to things that are familiar to us.

With no idea of what the future might bring.

God has created each person unique. And God has an amazing plan for you just as He did for Tebow, who uses his fame in football and baseball (minor league outfielder, New York Mets) to influence people to know Jesus.

Right now, when you don't know what the future holds for you, is the best time to begin to *stand strong*—to build a foundation of faith that will direct you to use your life in a way that honors God and gives you the best opportunity for true happiness in the future.

That's why we've put together this book, *Stand Strong for Boys*. We want to help you on your journey to fulfilling the plans God has for you.

Here's a little peek at what the book offers for each day as you begin to use it to help you stand strong.

- Bible passage. Look it up and read it. It'll give you some background for the lesson each day.
- Memory verse. Think about it for a moment or two before you read—and maybe go back and try to memorize it when you're done.
- The main article. It begins with a story or fact you can relate to. Then there's some biblical teaching and a challenge to grow in your faith and in your walk with Jesus.
- Fun fact. Additional interesting information about something in the article.
- A prayer. This can help you talk to God about the biblical teaching in the article.

That's it.

Five minutes a day to help you grow stronger!

It's not easy to stand strong for God these days. Actually, it's never been easy. But you can do it! And if you do—if you live in a way that glorifies God—you will be so glad you did!

STAND STRONG
FOR BOYS

90 FAITH-BUILDING DEVOTIONS

1
HELPING YOU STAND STRONG
2 TIMOTHY 4:1-8

I have fought the good fight, I have finished the race, I have kept the faith.

2 TIMOTHY 4:7

Back when your grandparents were young, if people had to live apart from each other for jobs or school, they had two ways to get in touch with each other: a long-distance phone call or a letter. The letter was cheaper, so that was often the way they communicated. It was exciting for them to go to the mailbox and find a letter from someone they hadn't seen in months! Lots of news and encouragement.

That might give you a little idea about the letters that are now a part of our Bible. Those are books like Colossians and Ephesians and 1 and 2 Timothy. This was how Paul the apostle stayed in touch with Christians in faraway places. Often, Paul was in prison for preaching about Jesus, so the letters were important for the people who loved him.

One of those letters was written to Paul's "son in the faith," Timothy. Paul told him: "The time for my departure is near. I have fought the good fight, I have finished the race, I have kept the faith." (2 Timothy 4:6–7).

When we read the letters in the Bible from heroes of the Christian faith, we can see how courageous they were. Paul was Timothy's example of strength. When you're having a rough day, think of this letter from Paul and remember how faithful and strong he was.

JUST YOU AND GOD

"Dear God, it sounds really cool to be strong like Paul, but I'm not. Please give me courage as a Christian."

FUN FACT

According to the British Broadcasting Corporation (BBC), during World War I, up to twelve million letters a week were delivered to the soldiers.

2

SUIT UP

EPHESIANS 6:13-21

Put on the full armor of God, so that when the day of evil comes, you may be able to stand your ground, and after you have done everything, to stand.

EPHESIANS 6:13

When you start playing football, one thing that takes some getting used to is all that equipment you have to wear. Running around in a helmet, shoulder pads, and other protective items feels awkward and clumsy at first. But soon it all becomes like a familiar friend providing welcome protection. When a football player suits up, he relies on his equipment to protect against a dangerous opponent.

As a follower of Christ, you have a different kind of dangerous foe—a spiritual enemy who seeks your downfall. He is referred to as Satan or the devil. Fortunately, our Lord has provided us with protection from him, and He challenges us to suit up.

Ephesians 6:13 says, "Put on the full armor of God, so that when the day of evil comes, you may be able to stand your ground." Paul then describes our armor—helmet, breastplate, shield, sword, belt, and shoes. They represent relying on the Bible (v. 17), praying (v. 18), and telling others about Jesus (vv. 19–20). These are important pieces of armor. So suit up! The battle is on!

JUST YOU AND GOD

"I know I need you to protect me. Help me learn more about the Bible and how to live for you."

In his hand is the life of every creature and the breath of all mankind.

JOB 12:10

3

THE VARIETY OF CREATION

JOB 12:7-13

Think about the amazing features God placed in the animals He created. Job wrote about several of them, including the ostrich. Despite its apparent lack of good sense and its odd parenting skills, its chicks survive (39:13-16). And despite its membership in the bird family, it can't fly—but it can outrun a horse (v. 18).

Another remarkable creature is the bombardier beetle. This African insect shoots two common materials, hydrogen peroxide and hydroquinone, from twin storage tanks in its back, blinding its attackers. A special nozzle inside the beetle mixes the chemicals, enabling it to bombard its foe at amazing speeds! The little guy can rotate his "cannon" to fire in any direction.

How can this be? How is it that a rather dull-witted ostrich survives although it's not very good at caring for its young while the bombardier beetle needs a complicated chemical reaction to make sure it survives? It's because God's creative abilities have no limits. "At his command they were created," the psalmist tells us (148:5). God's creative work is clear for everyone to see.

FUN FACT

Did you know that the wood frog actually freezes solid in the winter? Some important body parts are protected by a natural anti-freeze chemical. The rest? Solid as a rock all winter! Spring comes, it thaws out, and all is well.

JUST YOU AND GOD

"Lord, I keep hearing people tell me that you didn't create these things. They say it all evolved. Help me to keep believing in you."

4

ALL SAFE! ALL WELL!

HEBREWS 11:8-16

Now faith is confidence in what we hope for and assurance about what we do not see.

HEBREWS 11:1

On April 24, 1916, twenty-two men watched as Ernest Shackleton and five others set out in a tiny lifeboat for South Georgia, an island eight hundred miles away, to look for help. These twenty-eight men had reached ice-covered, mountainous Elephant Island after their ship *Endurance* was destroyed near Antarctica.

The odds of Shackleton's mission succeeding seemed impossible. If those six men could not find South Georgia—their only hope—all twenty-eight would certainly die. Imagine the joy of the twenty-two left behind when more than *four months later* a rescue boat appeared on the horizon with Shackleton on its bow shouting, "Are you all well?" And the call came back, "All safe! All well!"

What kept those men alive? Faith and hope placed in one man. They believed Shackleton would find a way to save them.

This human example of hope sounds like the faith of the heroes listed in Hebrews 11. Their faith in what the writer called "substance of things hoped for, the evidence of things not seen" kept people like Noah, Abraham, and Moses going during great difficulties (Hebrews 11:1 NKJV).

No matter what happens, you can have hope through your faith in one Man: Jesus.

JUST YOU AND GOD

"I'm trying to have faith, God. Sometimes it's hard because of what people say or because of bad things. Help me keep having faith in you!"

5

SHAQ AND ME

PSALM 111

The fear of the LORD is the beginning of wisdom.

PSALM 111:10

Imagine having your picture taken with Hall of Fame NBA player Shaquille O'Neal. Even if you are taller than all your friends, you'll be VERY short next to Shaq, who is over seven feet tall. You'll find out you aren't as tall as you thought you were.

Did you ever think of how much greater God is than we are? Sometimes we walk around like we're all that. But then we read that we don't know anything until we fear God first. One of the Psalms writers said, "The fear of the LORD is the beginning of wisdom" (111:10), or, "Wisdom begins with respect for the Lord" (ICB).

When we begin to respect God for all the amazing things He has done (maybe start with, say, *creating the universe*!), we start to get a better picture of how big God is.

So here's the deal. If we learn to know God more and love Him more because He is so much greater than we are, we'll begin to see how much we need to trust Him for everything!

It's pretty smart to realize how little we are next to God and how much we need Him and His great wisdom.

FUN FACT

When Shaquille was ten years old, he was already six feet, two inches tall!

JUST YOU AND GOD

"I know you are great, God, because you created everything. Thanks for still loving me, even though I'm just a kid."

6

MOUNTAINS AND TEMPLES

ZECHARIAH 4:1-7

"What are you, mighty mountain? Before Zerubbabel you will become level ground. Then he will bring out the capstone to shouts of 'God bless it! God bless it!'"

ZECHARIAH 4:7

Dashrath Manjhi and his friends had a problem.

His community in India stood next to a mountain—and that mountain kept his friends and family from getting to the hospital or buying supplies on the other side.

So here's what Dashrath did. He took a sledgehammer and some spikes, and he began chipping away. Twenty-two years later, he was done, and there was a passageway from his community to the city on the other side. He cut a gap in the mountain and built a path through it—with just a hammer, spikes, and his bare hands.

Now let's think about another builder with a big job to do. His name was Zerubbabel. He wasn't going to chop up a mountain. His job was to rebuild Israel's magnificent temple in Jerusalem, which had been destroyed by Nebuchadnezzar (lots of tough names today, right?).

Rebuilding it must have looked impossible. But Zerubbabel had help: the Holy Spirit's power (look up Zechariah 4:6). Zerubbabel trusted that God would help him (v. 7). And He did.

When there's a "mountain" before us, we have two choices: rely on our own strength or trust God to help us. When we trust Him, He'll either get the mountain out of our way or give us the strength to climb over it.

JUST YOU AND GOD

"Dear God, I'm not sure how to trust the Holy Spirit. So I'm praying that I can feel His presence today as I try to do my best for you."

FUN FACT

The mountain gap Dashrath created was 360 feet long, 30 feet wide, and 25 feet deep.

7

BIG UNIVERSE, GREAT GOD

PSALM 139:1-18

You know when I sit down and when I get up. You know my thoughts before I think them.

PSALM 139:2 ICB

Our universe is amazing! Did you know that the moon is spinning around us at nearly 2,300 miles an hour? That's slow compared to our Earth, which is spinning around the sun at 66,000 MPH. And our universe is so big that our sun, which is ninety-three million miles away from us, is one of 200 billion other stars. And there are trillions more planets in our galaxy.

Wow! Our little Earth (which has a surface area of about 197 million square miles) is no bigger than a pebble in our vast universe! How small does that make us?

Yet you don't have to feel small. You are important to God!

According to the Bible, the God of the galaxies pays attention to each microscopic one of us. He saw us before we existed (Psalm 139:13-16); He watches us as we go about our days, and He listens for our every thought (vv. 1-6).

When King David wrote Psalm 139, he was in a crisis (vv. 19-20). But he knew that God cared for him in a close, personal way: "You know when I sit down and when I get up," David told God (v. 2 ICB).

The One who created the vast universe knows you. That can help you get through one of those days when you feel kind of puny.

JUST YOU AND GOD

"Dear Father, I do feel small sometimes—like I don't matter that much. But I'm going to trust you. You said you know all about me—and you care."

While we were God's enemies, God made us his friends through the death of his Son.

ROMANS 5:10 ICB

WORK THINGS OUT

2 CORINTHIANS 5:16-21

Do you know about Dr. Martin Luther King Jr.? Dr. King was an American hero who helped bring equality and fairness to a group of people who were terribly mistreated.

Way back in 1957, as he prepared to preach one Sunday morning, he struggled. The unfair treatment of Black people made him struggle with the temptation to fight back.

But here's what he said to the people at the church where he preached that morning: "How do you go about loving your enemies?" he asked. "Begin with yourself. . . . When the opportunity presents itself for you to defeat your enemy, that is the time which you must not do it."

Quoting Jesus, King said: "Love your enemies, bless them that curse you, do good to them that hate you, and pray for them which despitefully use you" (Matthew 5:44 KJV). He wanted to change things for the better, but he knew it had to be done God's way.

Do you ever have to deal with kids who want to hurt you or make fun of you? Here's a verse that might help: But "[God] gave us the ministry of reconciliation" (2 Corinthians 5:18). This big word *reconciliation* means we "work things out" with people—not attack them. That's always what Jesus did.

Jesus, who was kind and compassionate, wants us to "work things out" too. Jesus wants us to love even those who don't seem to like us.

FUN FACT

At birth, Martin's name was Michael King. But his dad was so inspired by the story of reformer Martin Luther on a trip to Germany that he changed his name to Martin Luther King Sr. and his son's name to Martin Luther King Jr.

JUST YOU AND GOD

"If someone doesn't like me, Lord, what should I do? Help me to find the right adult to ask for help with this."

T-BALL FAITH

LUKE 15:1-7

The joy of the LORD is your strength.

NEHEMIAH 8:10

T-ball is a great version of baseball. It gives everyone the fun and joy of baseball before having to suffer the disappointment of striking out.

You've probably played T-ball, but in case you haven't, here is how it works. A baseball is placed on a rubber tee about waist-high to five- and six-year-old batters. Players swing until they hit the ball, and then they run.

Here is how one coach described what happened on his first night as a coach. The first batter hit the ball far into the outfield. Suddenly every player from every position ran to get the ball instead of staying where they were supposed to. When one of them reached it, there was nobody left in the infield for him to throw it to! All the players stood together—cheering excitedly!

Cheering is good! For instance, if you have recently come to know Jesus as Savior, a lot of people cheered for you. People were excited, and so were the angels in heaven! (It says so in Luke 15:7.) When you first meet Jesus, you are in love with God and excited about being in His family.

It's good to be excited about being a Christian! Your friends might see how happy you are and want to join you.

JUST YOU AND GOD

"I think it's really cool to be a Christian. It's pretty neat that angels get excited about new Christians. Thanks for saving me."

10

DOG TIRED?

MARK 2:23-28

Heaven belongs to the Lord. But he gave the earth to people.

PSALM 115:16 ICB

During the long, harsh Alaskan winter, Denali National Park rangers rely on teams of sled dogs to help them patrol the vast, snowy wilderness. Because Alaskan huskies live to run and pull, the dogs are always raring to go.

Those furry bundles of energy don't know when to stop, so park rangers have to make them rest. Otherwise, they'd run themselves until they collapse.

Sled dogs can remind us of our need to take a break. All of us—even if we are young—need to stop, rest, and recharge. You can't do school all day, practice basketball until dark, do your homework, and not expect to be tired. The biblical word for the rest God provides is *sabbath*. Jesus explained that the Sabbath "was made for man." It's not some complicated religious rule to follow (Mark 2:27).

After God made the universe, He "rested" on the seventh day (Genesis 2:2). This doesn't mean God was tired and needed a day off. He rested by enjoying the kingdom He had completed.

Let's do some Sabbath. Slow down and take a much-needed rest. It's more than taking a break; it's a way to spend time with God—who is in charge of this world.

FUN FACT

Denali National Park (DNP) contains 9,492 square miles of wilderness. DNP is larger than seven different US states: Vermont, New Hampshire, New Jersey, Hawaii, Connecticut, Delaware, and Rhode Island.

JUST YOU AND GOD

"Thanks, Lord, for rest. I love to sleep in! Help me to take some time to spend with you today."

11

AN AMAZING TREASURE

2 CORINTHIANS 4:1-7

We have this treasure from God. But we are only like clay jars that hold the treasure This shows that this power is from God, not from us.

2 CORINTHIANS 4:7 ICB

In March 1974, Chinese farmers who were digging a well made a shocking discovery: Buried under the dry ground of central China was what we now call the Terracotta Army—life-size sculptures that dated back 2,200 years! Amazingly, there were statues of some 8,000 soldiers, 150 cavalry horses, and 130 chariots drawn by 520 horses—all still intact! This has become a popular tourist site in China; more than a million visitors see it each year. This amazing treasure had been underground for twenty-two centuries!

Speaking of treasures—you have one inside you if you are a Christian. In 2 Corinthians 4:7, the apostle Paul wrote: "We have the treasure of the good news in these earthly bodies of ours" (NIRV). The treasure inside us is the message of Christ and His love, and we are supposed to tell others about it.

God wants other people to be welcomed into His family. Can you share that treasure with your friends?

FUN FACT

It took 700,000 workers to construct the Terracotta Army—plus a huge burial building for the emperor Qin Shi Huang. The whole thing took thirty-eight years to build.

JUST YOU AND GOD

"I am really grateful, Lord, that you saved me. It's not easy to tell others about this, so I need your help."

12

"NOT MY KIND"

GALATIANS 3:19-29

There is neither Jew nor Gentile, neither slave nor free, nor is there male and female, for you are all one in Christ Jesus.

GALATIANS 3:28

In the original Star Wars trilogy, there's a scene that can remind us of some church people. At a place to eat somewhere in a far corner of the galaxy, odd-looking creatures chat over food and music. When Luke Skywalker enters with his two droids, C-3PO and R2-D2 (who are more "normal" than anyone else there), he is surprisingly turned away: "We don't serve their kind here!" they are told.

That strange scene captures a problem we all struggle with—getting along with others. We feel more relaxed with people who are just like us.

Those of us who follow Christ should never say, "They're not my kind." Paul reminds us that we "are all one in Christ Jesus" (Galatians 3:28). So even if someone has a different attitude, race, or social standing, it shouldn't matter to us as Christians.

Here's an idea. If you find someone who is "not your kind," tell that person about Jesus!

JUST YOU AND GOD

"Lord, help me to think that no one is 'not my kind' and treat everyone the way you would want me to.

There is one thing I always do: I forget the things that are past. I try as hard as I can to reach the goal that is before me.

PHILIPPIANS 3:13-14 ICB

13

DISTRACTION

PHILIPPIANS 3:1-21

Students at a large university have a clever way of irritating opposing basketball players during free throws. They place a "curtain of distraction" behind the basket. Just before the free-throw attempts, the students open the curtain to show things like dancing unicorns or a lion wearing a tutu. Once, it was US Olympic swimmer Michael Phelps wearing his gold medals while pretending to swim.

The player missed *both* free throws.

These fun antics can remind us of how Satan distracts us. Sometimes he uses good things. For example, there is nothing wrong with many video games. But when they suck up our time and distract us from Jesus, that's not good. Maybe it's a sport that we spend all of our time playing, so that we're ignoring other good things we should do.

We all need to press on toward being godly and caring for others.

Sure, we can do fun things, but they should not distract us from the best things. Keep your eyes on Jesus!

FUN FACT

A guy named Blake Ahearn has the best free-throw shooting percentage in NCAA college basketball history. Playing for Missouri State from 2004 to 2007, he had a percentage of .9457. He made 435 out of 460 free throws. He played in nineteen games in the NBA (Miami, San Antonio, and Utah).

JUST YOU AND GOD

"I love to have fun, Lord. And I really want to serve you. Can you help me balance those two things in my life?"

14

FOLLOW ME

MARK 3:13-19

*"Come, follow me,"
Jesus said, "and I will
send you out to fish
for people." At once
they left their nets
and followed him.*

MARK 1:17-18

When the United States began its space program in 1958, seven men were chosen to become the first astronauts. Imagine the excitement of Scott Carpenter, Gordon Cooper, John Glenn, Gus Grissom, Walter Schirra, Alan Shepard, and Deke Slayton. They were chosen to go where no one had ever gone before—outer space!

They knew they would face new dangers and challenges. The thrill of being picked was tempered with the fear of the unknown. In fact, one of them, Gus Grissom, died in 1967 when a fire broke out in a command module.

Think of another set of men who were chosen for a vital mission: the twelve men Jesus chose as His disciples. These men left behind their jobs and families to follow a radical new teacher. They didn't know what kind of scary challenges they would face. Yet they joined up with Jesus.

Jesus is still asking us to join Him. He asks us to follow Him, love Him, obey Him, and tell others about Him. Like the apostles, we don't know what our commitment to Jesus might bring, but we know the rewards are great.

JUST YOU AND GOD

"Lord, help me to follow you faithfully and trust you completely. I wonder what kind of disciple I would have been."

15

DINGO THE DOG

PHILIPPIANS 2:1-4

*Do not be interested only in
your own life, but be interested
in the lives of others.*

PHILIPPIANS 2:4 ICB

Harry Tupper is a fishing legend in Idaho. There's a spot on Henry's Lake over on the east side of the state that's named for him: "Tupper's Hole."

What many people remember most about Harry, aside from fishing prowess, was his dog, Dingo. Now there was a dog! Dingo sat alongside Harry in his boat and watched intently while he fished. When Harry hooked a trout, Dingo would bark furiously until the fish was netted and released.

Dingo's enthusiasm teaches us something: It's better to get more excited about what others are doing than what we are doing.

Read Philippians 2:4 and think about Dingo. Then ask yourself: Do I spend time thinking about "the interests of others"? My friends? My parents? My brothers or sisters? Do I get as excited about what God is doing for others?

We are most like God when put others first. Paul said, "Give more honor to others than to yourselves" (2:3 ICB). Be like Dingo!

JUST YOU AND GOD

"Dear God, I need your help with this. I want to tell my friends that they are special. Help me to figure out how to do that."

16

WHAT COULD GO WRONG?

ACTS 9:1-19

Saul has seen a vision. In it a man named Ananias comes to him and lays his hands on him. Then he sees again.

ACTS 9:12 ICB

A high school student had a job at a bowling alley. It was early Saturday morning, and he was eager to get back to work. The evening before, he had stayed late to mop the floors because the janitor called in sick. He hadn't told his boss about the janitor; he wanted to show him he could do the work himself. After all, *What could go wrong?*

Plenty, it turns out.

Opening the door, the teen saw standing water—with bowling pins and other stuff bobbing on top. He realized what he had done: *He had left a large faucet running overnight!* Surprisingly, his boss greeted him with a huge hug and a big smile—"for trying," he said.

In Acts we read about Saul, who hated Christians. He hated and mistreated them (Acts 9:1–2)—until Jesus saved him on the road to Damascus (vv. 3–4). Saul was blinded by the experience, but guess who stepped in to help him? A Christian named Ananias. With God's help, he restored the sight of Saul, who became the great missionary Paul.

Both Paul and the teenager at the bowling alley received *unexpected* grace.

Can you show grace to someone today? Give a big smile and a kind word to a person who doesn't deserve it.

FUN FACT

Do you like bowling? There are 3,400 bowling alleys in the United States, and each year sixty-seven million people go bowling.

JUST YOU AND GOD

"Dear God, I like that word grace. Please help me show grace to my friends when they are acting like jerks?"

Everyone who hears these things I say and obeys them is like a wise man. The wise man built his house on rock.

MATTHEW 7:24 ICB

17
FOLLOW THE INSTRUCTIONS?

MATTHEW 7:24-29

There are a couple of ways to build model planes. One is for guys who don't think they need instructions. That is, until they glue some pieces together and realize they skipped a key step, like putting the pilot in the cockpit! The other way—reading the instructions first—usually works better.

It's easy to think we don't need instructions in life, either—only to later realize that we've messed things up.

Jesus said that following His instructions allow wise people to build a good life (Matthew 7:24-27). He said, "Everyone who hears these things I say and obeys them is like a wise man. The wise man built his house on rock" (v. 24 ICB).

People who don't follow His instructions, Jesus said, are "foolish" (v. 26). Forgiving others, helping the poor, and obeying your parents may seem to some of your buddies like a silly way to build a life. But take it from Jesus, that's the way to go.

FUN FACT

Among the most popular plastic model airplanes are the WWII fighter-bomber 51D Mustang and the A-10 Warthog, which was used in Desert Storm in the 1990s. Look them up online. They are really cool airplanes!

JUST YOU AND GOD

"Lately, dear heavenly Father, I have been trying to live for you. Give me more courage to know exactly what that means?"

18

PISTOL PETE'S SEARCH

MATTHEW 16:24-28

It is worth nothing for a man to have the whole world if he loses his soul.

MATTHEW 16:26 ICB

Pistol Pete Maravich was one of basketball's all-time great players. While at LSU, Maravich averaged 44.2 points per game—the highest average in NCAA history. Then during his NBA career, he became one of the top fifty players in league history.

Yet this incredible basketball player was not happy.

Pete wrote in his journal: "I pray that before I'm through with this entire life of mine, I will be happy, peaceful, and my mind at ease about life and God. How can I be unhappy? It is very simple. There are millions of people who have not found a deep sense of purpose and meaning. I am one of them. . . . With all the trophies, awards, money, and fame; I am not at peace with myself."

Five years after Maravich wrote those words, he found the peace he wanted—peace that came when he cried out to God pleading for forgiveness, saying, "Jesus, I know you're real. . . . I've got nowhere to go. If you don't save me, I won't last two more days."

At that moment, Pete's life changed forever. "When I took God into my heart, it was the first true happiness I ever had."

The Lord gave Maravich peace through faith in Jesus. Have you asked Jesus to do the same for you?

JUST YOU AND GOD

"I don't know much about this Pistol Pete guy, Lord, but I'm glad you saved him and saved me!"

19

FROM FAILURE TO SUCCESS

ACTS 12:24-13:13

*I can do all this through him
who gives me strength.*

PHILIPPIANS 4:13

You know who Thomas Edison was, right? The guy who invented the light bulb.

Well, one night he was working late in his laboratory. At two o'clock in the morning, an assistant came in and noticed that the inventor was smiling broadly. "Have you solved the problem?" he asked. "No," replied Edison. "That experiment didn't work at all. Now I can start over again." Edison could say that because he realized that each failure brought him a little closer to finding the right answer.

This is not a new idea. In New Testament days Mark had joined Paul and Barnabas on their first missionary journey to Cyprus (an island in the Mediterranean Sea) and Perga (which is in the country of Turkey), but then he left them. It looked like Mark had failed. But he was willing to try again. So he became an important helper for Barnabas on a later trip to Cyprus. Still later, when Paul was in a Roman dungeon, he asked for Mark, whom he called "helpful" (2 Timothy 4:11), to visit him.

Have you had a major fail? Don't let it stop you. Learn from it and move ahead. Trust God to give you strength. Use that failure as a step toward success.

FUN FACT

When Thomas Edison was in school, one of his teachers said he was "too stupid to learn anything." Wonder what she thought when one day she could turn on an electric light that her "stupid" student invented!

JUST YOU AND GOD

"God, when I mess up (which is too often), remind me that you love me and want to help me do better."

20

TOUGH TREES

ROMANS 5:1-5

We also have joy with our troubles because we know that these troubles produce patience. And patience produces character, and character produces hope.

ROMANS 5:3-4 ICB

Bristlecone pines are the Earth's oldest living trees. Some are estimated to be 3,000 to 4,000 years old (that's up to 2,000 years before Jesus was born!). Another tree, Methuselah, is 4,850 years old! It was old when the Egyptians built the pyramids.

Bristlecones grow atop some mountains of the western United States at elevations of 10,000 to 11,000 feet. They've survived some of the harshest living conditions on Earth: arctic temperatures, fierce winds, thin air, and little rainfall.

Their brutal environment is one of the reasons they've survived. Hardship has produced great strength and staying power in those old trees.

Do you think that might work for people? The apostle Paul says yes! He said that troubles lead to patience, which teaches us character (Romans 5:3-4). God can use the tough things we have to go through to make us stronger. If we lean on Jesus because of a bad event, it can become a good thing.

Let's say you had a bad day. After you pray for God's help, then ask Him to make something good come of the crummy stuff you had to go through. Then you'll have hope. And that's what makes you want to start all over again tomorrow!

JUST YOU AND GOD

"It's pretty cool, God, that the Bible says that even after trouble comes, good things follow later. I need to remember that."

We have troubles all around us, but we are not defeated. We do not know what to do, but we do not give up.

2 CORINTHIANS 4:8 ICB

21
CHOOSING THE HARD THING
2 CORINTHIANS 4:5-18

On September 12, 1962, President John F. Kennedy delivered a speech at Rice University in Houston, Texas. He set a big goal for the United States: to put a man on the moon.

Kennedy said, "We choose to go to the moon in this decade [meaning during the 1960s]. We choose to go to the moon and do the other things, not because they are easy but because they are hard." The nation responded. Less than seven years later, on July 20, 1969, millions of people around the world watched on TV as Neil Armstrong took "one giant leap for mankind" by walking on the surface of the moon.

We all need challenges! We become better when we try to do hard things.

The apostle Paul found that serving Jesus was sometimes hard, but that wasn't a reason to stop. He kept his focus on Christ, and he wrote, "We have troubles all around us, but we are not defeated! . . . We do not give up!" (2 Corinthians 4:8 ICB). The goal is worth the hard work.

With God's help, we can serve Jesus every day—not just when it's easy but also when it's hard.

JUST YOU AND GOD

"Dear God, have you seen my homework list? It's hard to get all of that done! Especially my _____ assignments. I don't want to give up, but I need some help."

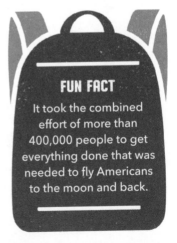

FUN FACT

It took the combined effort of more than 400,000 people to get everything done that was needed to fly Americans to the moon and back.

22

KEEP RUNNING!

HEBREWS 12:1-3

*Let us run the race that is before
us and never give up.*

HEBREWS 12:1 ICB

John Stephen Akhwari, a marathon runner from Tanzania, finished last at the 1968 Olympics in Mexico City. No last-place finisher in a marathon ever finished quite so last.

Injured along the way, he hobbled into the stadium more than an hour after the other runners had com-

pleted the race. Only a few spectators were left in the stands when Akhwari finally crossed the finish line. When asked why he continued to run despite the pain, Akhwari replied, "My country did not send me to Mexico City to start the race. They sent me here to finish."

That's a great attitude! The person who wrote the book of Hebrews says that there is a "race marked out for us" (Hebrews 12:1), and we are to keep running until we reach the finish line. You've started your race, so now keep on running.

Along the way, you may get a bit hobbled. Maybe have some problems or even some doubts. But God asks for you to keep going. Keep running for Jesus!

You've got a long road ahead. So make a pact with God that you'll do your best for Him. And just keep going for Him on the race marked out for you.

JUST YOU AND GOD

"God, I've seen older kids at church turn against you. Please help me never to do that."

23

NEVER ALONE

HEBREWS 13:1-8

Keep your lives free from the love of money and be content with what you have, because God has said, "Never will I leave you; never will I forsake you."

HEBREWS 13:5

Many people who have played soccer have a lifelong love for "The Beautiful Game." One of the top leagues is the English Premier League—where the skill and speed with which the game is played is high-level. One of the cool things fans of some of those teams do is that they sing in support of their beloved "sides." For instance, Liverpool has for years had "You'll Never Walk Alone" as its theme. It's pretty moving to hear 50,000 fans rise as one to sing that old standard! It's an encouragement to players and fans alike that they will see each other through to the end. Walk alone? Never.

Even at your age, you don't like to go it alone. You need your buddies to talk to and do stuff with. It can be lonely if nobody's around to hang out with. Remember the Coronavirus quarantine?

But here's something to think about: As a Christian, you never need to fear abandonment. God has told us, "Never will I leave you; never will I forsake you" (Hebrews 13:5). That's even better than the Liverpool song! It is the promise of God himself to those who are the objects of His love. He is there—and He isn't going away.

With Christ by your side, you will never walk alone.

JUST YOU AND GOD

"I see what the Bible says about never being alone, but sometimes I feel like I am. I need you to help me know what it means that you will never leave me."

24

THIRTY-FIVE MILLION BEATS

JOB 38:1–11

*From birth I have relied
on you; you brought
me forth from my
mother's womb.
I will ever praise you.*

PSALM 71:6

What do you do a hundred thousand times a day and never even think about it? You pump blood with your heartbeat. That adds up to thirty-five million beats in your lifetime by about the time you start sixth grade. Or, to make you even more tired, if you live to be an average age, that heart of yours will have pounded out two and a half *billion* beats.

Yet as amazing as our heart is, it's just one example in the natural world of something that's designed to tell us about our Creator. This is the idea behind the true story of a man named Job.

Broken by some horrible tragedies in his life, Job felt abandoned. When God finally spoke to him, He didn't tell Job why bad things were happening. Instead, He drew Job's attention to some natural wonders—telling us about a power far greater than our own (Job 38:1-11). God's power.

So what can we learn from this hardworking muscle, the heart? The message may be similar to the sound of a thunderstorm or the sight of the constellations in the sky (which God told Job about). The amazing power and creative wisdom of God tell us that we can trust Him for everything in life. Do you trust Him?

FUN FACT

Job 38:31 mentions two constellations: Pleiades and Orion. Pleiades is sometimes called the Seven Sisters. It is one of the most visible star clusters in the sky.

JUST YOU AND GOD

"Jesus, I want to trust you with my whole heart. But sometimes I have doubts and fears. I need you to remind me somehow that you care."

25

THE WORST DEFEAT

2 KINGS 25:1-21

All this happened in Jerusalem and Judah because the Lord was angry with them. Finally, he threw them out of his presence.

2 KINGS 24:20 ICB

There have been some horrible defeats in sports history, but none worse than Cumberland's 222-0 loss to Georgia Tech in 1916. It was the worst college football defeat ever, and the Cumberland players must have been devastated.

Another kind of loss happened to the people of Jerusalem in 586 BC—much worse than any sports defeat. Because of their disobedience, God allowed them to be defeated by the Babylonian army (2 Kings 24:20).

Led by Nebuchadnezzar, the Babylonians left the Holy City in ruins. They burned the majestic temple, the palace of the king, and the people's homes. And the people were led away to live in Babylon—1,600 miles away.

It was one of the worst defeats in the history of God's people, the Jews. Their continued disobedience had terrible consequences. Through it all, God urged them to repent and turn back to Him.

God really wants us to live in a way that honors Him! We should live as God wants us to live—just because of how much it means to Him.

Jerusalem's loss can challenge us to live in obedience to God.

JUST YOU AND GOD
"God, it's amazing that the people of Israel got to go back home. I know you like to forgive people. I need that sometimes."

He will wipe every tear from their eyes. There will be no more death or mourning or crying or pain, for the old order of things has passed away.

REVELATION 21:4

26

THE TRAIL OF TEARS

REVELATION 21:1-7

A tragic event in US history was the forced move of thousands of Native Americans in the nineteenth century. Their tribes were driven out of lands they had lived on for hundreds of years. In the winter of 1838, thousands of Cherokee were forced to take a brutal 1,000-mile march known as the Trail of Tears to a new home in Oklahoma. This resulted in the deaths of thousands of people.

There's still a lot of pain and heartache in our world. Bad things happen to families, and sometimes a family member dies. Our Lord sees our tears and comforts our sad hearts (2 Corinthians 1:3-5). He also tells us about a future time when there won't be any sin or injustice anymore. In heaven, "God will wipe away every tear from their eyes; there shall be no more death" (Revelation 21:4 NKJV).

God not only offers freedom from tears in the future but He also can help us through our troubles now.

FUN FACT

A Cherokee scholar named Sequoyah created an alphabet and a writing system for his tribe, which meant the people could read and write their own language.

JUST YOU AND GOD

"I like it, God, that when you thought up heaven, you decided there would be no tears. I can't wait!"

27

BRING IT ON!

2 CORINTHIANS 11:22-12:10

I have been in danger from rivers, from thieves, from my own people, the Jews, and from those who are not Jews. I have been in danger in cities, in places where no one lives, and on the sea.

2 CORINTHIANS 11:26 ICB

A program on the History channel showed the world's most extreme airports. The program mentioned one airport I had landed in before. That Asian airport was a thrill ride for passengers and a challenge for pilots. If you came in from one direction, you had to fly over skyscrapers and then hope the plane stopped before it plunged into the sea. If you came in the other way, it seemed as if you were going to smack into a mountain.

One pilot who used to take planeloads of people into that airport before it was shut down and replaced said, "I miss flying into that airport." As a pilot, he looked forward to the challenge.

Sometimes we run from challenges, don't we? But think about this: The people we love to read about in the Bible are impressive because they faced challenges. Think about Paul. With the confidence of God's help, he faced troubles head-on. Jesus's promise to Paul—and to us—is this: "My grace is enough for you. When you are weak, then my power is made perfect in you" (2 Corinthians 12:9 ICB). Because of Jesus, when you have a tough test or some other challenge, you can say: Bring it on!

JUST YOU AND GOD

"Can I pray a verse back to you, Lord? 'Your grace is enough for me. When I am weak, your power is made perfect in me.'"

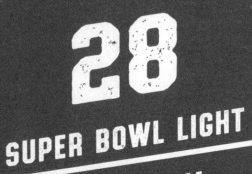

28

SUPER BOWL LIGHT

EPHESIANS 5:8-14

For you were once darkness, but now you are light in the Lord. Live as children of light.

EPHESIANS 5:8

For many years a Christian reporter attended the Super Bowl to get interviews with athletes for his Christian radio program.

He said that when he first started covering the game, he didn't like the atmosphere of Super Bowl week. "It was a very dark place," he said—talking about how it was spiritually.

One day he told a former NFL player, a Christian, how he was feeling. The football player told him, "Brother, you are being light in this dark place." That comment reminded my friend why he was there, and it helped him grow excited about serving God in a place where the light of the gospel of Jesus Christ is needed. He knew he had to shine his light.

Perhaps you have to go to school in a place where you can't talk about God and where your friends sometimes mock you for being a "Jesus guy." Maybe it feels like "a very dark place." Or maybe you take Taekwondo or golf lessons where there aren't any other Christians.

Ask God for help! You can be a light (Ephesians 5:8)—through your smiles, kind words and actions, and hard work. You may be the only light other kids see today.

JUST YOU AND GOD

"Sometimes, Lord, my friends can be such smart alecks. I want to be a light, but I'm afraid they'll just make fun of me. Help me with that."

29

YOU'RE NOT HOME YET

PHILIPPIANS 3:17-4:1

Our homeland is in heaven, and we are waiting for our Savior, the Lord Jesus Christ, to come from heaven.

PHILIPPIANS 3:20 ICB

Shortly after Theodore Roosevelt's presidency ended in 1909, he went on a hunting safari to Africa. When the former president returned to the United States after the safari, he was on the same ship as a missionary who was retiring after forty years of service for God in a remote jungle village. When the ship docked back home, a cheering crowd greeted Roosevelt, but not a single person was there to welcome the returning missionary.

At first, the missionary felt sorry for himself. He thought, *When a president comes home after a short hunting trip, hundreds come out to greet him. But Lord, when one of your missionaries comes home after a lifetime of service, no one is there to meet him.* Immediately he felt as if the Lord was saying to him, "But My son, you are not home yet."

What did this mean? It meant that this world we live in, as great as it is, is not all there is. Look at Philippians 3:20. As a Christian, your eternal citizenship is not of this world. Someday you'll receive the real welcome from God in heaven. Sounds pretty cool, right?

FUN FACT

Theodore Roosevelt, the twenty-sixth president of the United States, was an uncle of Eleanor Roosevelt, wife of the thirty-second president, Franklin Roosevelt.

JUST YOU AND GOD

"God, it is hard for me to imagine heaven. But I want to thank you for it, because I know some people there, and I know it'll be great for me someday."

*Happy is the person
who fears the Lord.*

PSALM 112:1 ICB

30

A GOOD MAN

PSALM 112

Who are the good men in your life? Perhaps your dad. Your grandpa. Your pastor. Maybe a favorite guy teacher at school. A sports coach.

At your age, this is a good time to seek out men you can trust to lead you to make good decisions and to live for Jesus in an exciting new way.

So how do you know what to look for in a good man?

In Psalm 112 we find a clear set of guidelines for what makes a man good. According to the psalmist, a good man *fears the Lord* (v. 1), *delights in God's commands* (v. 1), and is *gracious, compassionate, and righteous* (v. 4). He *is generous and makes good decisions* (v. 5). He is *unshakable in his faith*, and he has no fear because *his trust is in God* (vv. 6–8).

Looking for a good man to lead you in life? Reread Psalm 112. It gives you a pattern for all Christian men to follow if they want to make a difference in their world.

JUST YOU AND GOD

"Dear God in heaven. I know I'm just a kid, but I want to be like the person in Psalm 112. Will you help me?"

31

A PARADE OF ONE

MATTHEW 21:1-11

Your king is coming to you . . .
gentle and riding on a donkey.

ZECHARIAH 9:9 ICB

There are parades, and then there are PARADES!

You might think of a parade as the Christmas event in your town when Santa Claus rides on a float. Or maybe a Fourth of July parade with bands and local celebrities.

And then there are PARADES! In American history, the greatest parades focused on people such as Charles Lindbergh–the first person to fly solo across the Atlantic Ocean. Or the Apollo 11 astronauts, who were the first men to walk on the moon. These celebrations were marked by ticker-tape showers and crowds of adoring fans lining the streets of a major city as historically important people pass by.

But *the greatest parade ever* was quite different. It happened in Jerusalem two thousand years ago. It was a simple one-man donkey ride over a road covered with garments and palm branches.

Do you know what's truly amazing? The prophet Zechariah wrote about this parade five hundred years before it happened. He said, "Your king is coming to you . . . gentle and riding on a donkey" (9:9 ICB).

When Jesus rode that donkey into Jerusalem, He was giving us one more reason to shout, "Hosanna!" which means "God saves!" Whether in a parade or in our prayers, Jesus deserves our praise!

JUST YOU AND GOD

"Jesus, it would have been so cool to see you ride that donkey into Jerusalem! When I get to heaven, can we talk about what that was like?"

FUN FACT

News reports from the August 13, 1969, parade of Apollo 11 astronauts say that millions of people lined the streets of New York to see Michael Collins, Neil Armstrong, and Buzz Aldrin.

32

LITTLE NICKS—BIG TROUBLE

GALATIANS 5:7-9

A little yeast works through the whole batch of dough.

GALATIANS 5:9

They couldn't figure it out. A man and his son had bought an old powerboat for fishing but couldn't make it run properly. It couldn't get up to speed, and it began shaking when they tried to go faster. They adjusted the carburetor and changed the fuel filter, but that didn't help.

When they took the boat out of the water, the son found something. One of the propeller fins had a 3/4-inch nick in it. *That can't be it*, they thought. *That nick is too small.* But when they installed a new propeller, it purred like a new engine! They had been slowed down by a tiny nick.

Can you think of something similar in your life? What about little sins? Galatians 5:16–21 talks about a lot of sins that people get themselves into. And they usually start with something little. That's what Galatians 5:9 is talking about when it mentions yeast and dough (ask your mom what that's all about). If we ignore "little" sins, they'll eventually grow—maybe even harming people around us. Be careful, a "little" sin can mess up our relationship with Jesus and others.

Little nicks can cause big trouble.

JUST YOU AND GOD

"Sometimes I do little things that I know are wrong. Can you help me, Lord, to stop doing that? And can you forgive me for those things?"

33

HELP WITH A HOME RUN

1 PETER 4:7-11

Each of you should use whatever gift you have received to serve others, as faithful stewards of God's grace.

1 PETER 4:10

Sara Tucholsky, a softball player for Western Oregon University, hit a home run in a game against Central Washington. But it almost didn't count. As she rounded first base in excitement, she missed touching the base! Turning around to step on first, she badly twisted her knee. She fell to the ground in pain.

The rules say that for the home run to count, Sara would have to touch all four bases. And her teammates were not allowed to help her.

So Mallory Holtman, the first baseman for the opposing team, talked to the umpire. "Would it be okay if we carried her around?" she asked. The umpire said yes. So Mallory and another teammate made a chair of their hands and carted Sara around the bases so she could "touch 'em all." By the time they were through carrying her, many were crying at this selfless act of compassion. And Sara was awarded her home run!

What a lesson for us all. When we see someone stumble in life, we can follow the example of these ballplayers. Reach out. Lift others up and carry them along. That way, we "serve others, as faithful stewards of God's grace" (1 Peter 4:10).

FUN FACT

Lauren Chamberlain, who played for Oklahoma, has the all-time record for home runs in NCAA softball history. She hit ninety-five round-trippers for the Sooners from 2012 to 2015.

JUST YOU AND GOD

"Will you help me, Lord, to find a couple of people who need my help, and help me figure out what to do for them?"

My God will meet all your needs according to the riches of his glory in Christ Jesus.

PHILIPPIANS 4:19

34

WHAT ON EARTH?

MATTHEW 17:24-27

Andrew Cheatle lost his cell phone. He had been at the beach, and he was sure he'd never see it again.

About a week later, a fisherman named Glen Kerley called Andrew—on Andrew's phone! He had pulled the phone, still working after it dried out, from a twenty-five-pound cod! It sounds fishy, but it's true.

Life has a lot of odd stories. And so does the Bible!

One day some tax collectors came up to Peter and asked, "Doesn't your teacher [Jesus] pay the temple tax?" (Matthew 17:24). Well, He didn't really have to; He was of King of kings. Also, taxes weren't collected from the children of the king, so the Lord said neither He nor His followers (His "children") owed any temple tax (vv. 25-26).

But Jesus didn't want to offend anyone (v. 27), so He told Peter to go fishing. He did, and he found a coin in the mouth of the first fish he caught. They paid the tax with it.

What is Jesus doing here? He is the rightful King—and when we accept His role as Lord in our lives, we become His children.

Life will still throw its various demands at us, but Jesus showed that He can provide for us.

JUST YOU AND GOD

"It is so great to be considered as a part of your family. Help me to be a good rep of who you are to everyone I meet."

FUN FACT

It has been estimated that seventy million cellphones are lost every year, and about five million of them are never found.

35

ALONE IN SPACE

GENESIS 28:10-17

When Jacob awoke from his sleep, he thought, "Surely the LORD is in this place, and I was not aware of it."

GENESIS 28:16

Apollo 15 astronaut Al Worden was all by himself. Completely! For three days in 1971, he flew alone in his command module, *Endeavour*, around the moon while David Scott and James Irwin were exploring the lunar surface below. The next closest humans were 230,000 miles away on Earth.

You've heard of the Old Testament man named Jacob, right? Well he was all alone one time too. But for a different reason. He was on the run from his older brother, Esau, who wanted to kill him. They were fighting about something called the family blessing, which Jacob stole from Esau. It was a big deal in those days.

All by himself out in the countryside at night, Jacob fell asleep. He dreamed of a staircase going to heaven. As he watched angels going up and down, he heard God's voice. It promised that God would be with him and bless the whole earth through his children. When Jacob woke up, he said, "Surely the LORD is in this place" (Genesis 28:16).

Jacob was by himself because he had cheated his brother. But he wasn't really alone. God was still with him. Keep that in mind when you feel alone against the world. Talk to God; He's right there.

JUST YOU AND GOD

*"Lord, I feel alone in these situations: _____.
Please be with me and help me to know that
it's not just me. There are two of us."*

36

LEAP THE WALL

ROMANS 12:14-21

If your enemy is hungry, feed him; if he is thirsty, give him something to drink.

ROMANS 12:20

Sgt. Richard Kirkland was a Confederate (South) soldier in the US Civil War (1861–1865). During the Battle of Fredericksburg in late 1862, the Union Army (North) lost a skirmish at Marye's Heights, leaving wounded soldiers suffering in what is called no-man's-land (a place that neither side is controlling).

Kirkland got permission to help those men. Collecting canteens, he jumped over a stone wall and bent over the first soldier to help him. At great personal risk, the "Angel of Marye's Heights" (as he was later called) gave the mercy of Christ to enemy soldiers.

Here's hoping you never have to be on a battlefield. But even at your age, you will have the chance to help people. It could be a friend with problems at home or someone who seems to get picked on. "Leap the wall" and help the person!

The apostle Paul said, "If your enemy is hungry, feed him; if he is thirsty, give him something to drink" (Romans 12:20). So, whether the person who needs help is your friend or not, be an encouragement. Show Jesus's love to him or her.

Paul's challenge would be that we follow Sgt. Kirkland's example. Today is the day for us to "leap the wall" of safety to lend comfort from God to those in need.

JUST YOU AND GOD

"I like Sgt. Kirkland's story. Help me to be a little bit like him."

37

WAITING TO CHEER

EPHESIANS 3:14-21

Christ's love is greater than any person can ever know. But I pray that you will be able to know that love. Then you can be filled with the fullness of God.

EPHESIANS 3:19 ICB

In his first Little League baseball game, a player got hit in the face with a ball. He wasn't hurt but was understandably shaken. For the rest of the season, he was afraid of the ball. Game after game, he bravely kept batting, but he just couldn't hit the ball.

In his team's final game, his team was way behind when he stepped up to the plate for the last time in the season. Thwack! To everyone's surprise, he hit the ball sharply! Everyone—teammates and parents alike—cheered loudly. The coach was jumping up and down! Everyone loved this kid and cheered him on.

I imagine that the Lord cheers us on in our lives as well. He loves us deeply and desires that we may know "Christ's love," which "is greater than any person can ever know" (Ephesians 3:19 ICB).

By the way we live, we can show others about Jesus's deep love for us—and them. Think about how cool it will be when they hear that God loves them so much that He sent Jesus to die on the cross for their sin. And that He wants to cheer them on!

FUN FACT

One major league player who played Little League baseball is Cody Bellinger. He played in the Little League World Series in 2007 and hit a home run. In 2017, he hit a home run in the MLB World Series for the LA Dodgers.

JUST YOU AND GOD

"I know you have put people in my life who are cheering me on. Help me to remember to say thanks to them."

38

DRIFTING AWAY

2 CORINTHIANS 6:14-7:1

You are not the same as those who do not believe. So do not join yourselves to them. Good and bad do not belong together.

2 CORINTHIANS 6:14 ICB

Adrian Vasquez frantically waved from his tiny fishing boat. A cruise ship was within sight, and Adrian was trying to get the ship's attention.

After their boat's engine had failed, Adrian and two friends had been adrift—floating aimlessly—for days on the ocean. Some passengers on the cruise ship spotted Adrian's boat and told crewmembers. For some reason, though, the ship didn't stop to help. Adrian was finally rescued by a different ship *two weeks later.*

Back in the Bible days of the apostle Paul, people in the church at a city named Corinth seemed to be adrift. They were confused about how to live as Christians. So Paul "tossed them" what we might call the "life ring" of true faith in Jesus. Some of the people had been going to non-Christian religious services (1 Corinthians 10:14-22). They were even worshiping idols! So Paul asked, "What does a believer have in common with an unbeliever?" (2 Corinthians 6:15).

There's a big difference between people who have faith in Jesus and those who don't. Paul told his readers not to drift away from God but to stay close to shore by hanging on to their faith in Jesus.

Do you have a friend who's starting to drift away from Jesus? Don't just cruise by. Stop and help.

JUST YOU AND GOD

"Today, I'm concerned about my friend _____. Please make sure he doesn't drift away from you. Thank you."

39

WHAT'S A WINDTALKER?

2 PETER 1:19-21

No prophecy ever came from what a man wanted to say. But men led by the Holy Spirit spoke words from God.

2 PETER 1:21 ICB

Do you ever try to talk to your friends in code? Or make up a way to write notes to each other so no one else but you and your friends can read it?

That happens sometimes in war times. For instance, during World War II, the United States needed to come up with a code the enemies

couldn't read. The Marines recruited twenty-seven Navajo Native Americans to do this because they had a language no one else outside their small group had ever heard spoken. These men were called "windtalkers." And it worked! The code was never broken.

The Bible, on the other hand, is not some kind of impossible code. God wanted us to get His message. It was written by human authors to give people the news of God's love and salvation.

Although some parts are hard to understand, the message of the Bible is clear. "In the beginning God created the heavens and the earth" (Genesis 1:1). And, "For God so loved the world that he gave his one and only Son" (John 3:16). We know we were created by God, and we know we can be saved by Jesus.

Get going reading the Bible. No code-breaking needed.

JUST YOU AND GOD

"Sometimes, Lord, I try to read the Bible, but I don't understand it. Help me to find someone who can help me be better at it."

40

DOUBLE COVERAGE

PROVERBS 16

Stay away from everything that is evil.

1 THESSALONIANS 5:22 ICB

Have you ever played quarterback? Or if not, you've probably watched great quarterbacks like Drew Brees and Russell Wilson in action. And you probably know that one of the worst things they can do is to throw the ball into double coverage.

Quarterbacks would rather take a sack or toss the ball out of bounds than to pass to a player who's being shadowed by two defenders. It's too risky—and most likely will lead to an interception.

A football coach views a quarterback's pass into double coverage as an unnecessary evil. Almost nothing good can come from it!

The words of 1 Thessalonians 5:22 remind us as followers of Jesus Christ that we need to avoid real-life situations that are comparable to a quarterback throwing into double coverage. We need to avoid those things that are risky—and that includes everything that is sinful. We need to avoid throwing ourselves into situations where sin and unhealthy decisions can intercept us.

The next time you face a difficult decision or situation, think like a good quarterback and avoid double coverage. Be cautious. Stay away from everything that is evil.

JUST YOU AND GOD

"Sometimes my friends tell me it's okay to do bad things—just don't get caught. Can you help me figure out what to say to them?"

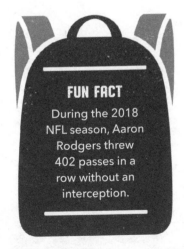

FUN FACT

During the 2018 NFL season, Aaron Rodgers threw 402 passes in a row without an interception.

41

CHECK THE COMPASS

JOHN 7:37-53

See if there is any bad thing in me.
Lead me in the way you set long ago.

PSALM 139:24 ICB

Two Florida men charted a course and drove their fishing boat out into the Gulf of Mexico. Using the boat's compass, they headed to deep waters sixty miles offshore where they hoped to catch some fish called groupers. When they arrived, they turned on their depth finder and realized they were nowhere near their

target. Oops. One of the men had laid a flashlight near the ship's compass, and the attached magnet had messed up the reading.

Just as that magnet changed the compass, so our sinful hearts can influence the way we think. Many people in Jesus's day, for example, thought they were moving in the right direction by refusing to think He was the Messiah (John 7:41–42). The "magnet" that threw off their thinking was bias (which means they already had feelings against Jesus). They were afraid Jesus would damage their religious traditions. They trusted their wrong beliefs. As a result, they plotted to kill the One who had come to save them.

We might have doubts too, and they may throw off our spiritual compass. With God's help, we can get back on course—trusting what He tells us in the Bible.

JUST YOU AND GOD

"Dear God, I know that the Bible is true, but it's hard to understand sometimes. Is it okay to tell you that? I need somebody to help me figure it out."

Christ died for us while we were still sinners. In this way God shows his great love for us.

ROMANS 5:8 ICB

42

SOLVING THE MYSTERY

ROMANS 5:1-11

One of the most popular places to visit in England is Stonehenge. Its massive pieces of granite are a great source of mystery. Every year, people travel to Stonehenge with questions such as: Why were they put there? Who built this? How did they do it? But visitors leave having received no answers from the silent stones. The mystery remains.

The Scriptures speak of a greater mystery—the fact that God came to live among us as a man: "Great is the mystery of godliness," Paul says (1 Timothy 3:16 NKJV). "He was shown to us in a human body, proved right by the Spirit, and seen by angels. He was preached to the nations, believed in by the world, and taken to heaven in glory" (v. 16 ICB).

This brief review of the life of Christ—the mystery of godliness—is amazing. What led to our Savior's great sacrifice, however, is not a mystery. "Christ died for us while we were still sinners. In this way God shows his great love for us" (Romans 5:8 ICB). God's great love solves the mystery of godliness. The cross has made it plain for everyone to see.

JUST YOU AND GOD

"God, thank you for letting me in on the story of Jesus. I am so glad that He saved me from my sin!"

43

STAR SHEPHERD

ISAIAH 40:25-27

Look up to the skies. Who created all these stars? He leads out all the army of heaven one by one. He calls all the stars by name. He is very strong and full of power. So not one of them is missing.

ISAIAH 40:26 ICB

Some night when you're away from city lights, "Look up to the skies" (Isaiah 40:26 ICB).

If you have good eyes, you can see about 5,000 stars, according to astronomer Simon Driver. There are, however, far more that you cannot see. The Hubble Deep Field Study space probe concluded that there are billions of galaxies, each containing billions of stars. By one estimate, there are more than ten stars in the universe for every grain of sand on the earth.

Yet each night, without fail, God "leads out all the army of heaven one by one. . . . He is very strong and full of power. So not one of them is missing" (v. 26 ICB).

If God sees all the stars, why do we sometimes say, "The Lord does not see what happens to me" (v. 27 ICB)? No one has been forgotten by God. He knows "those who are his" (2 Timothy 2:19). If He can bring out the billions of stars in the heaven each night one by one, He can keep His eye on you too!

Go look at the stars! Then praise the Lord! God cares for you too.

FUN FACT

Besides the sun, the closest star to earth is 4.3 light-years away from us (do you remember what a light-year is?). The closest star is in the Alpha Centauri star system.

JUST YOU AND GOD

"Wow, God. The sky is so amazing at night. I can't believe how many stars you created. Help me to see something in creation every day to thank you for."

44

BIG SPRING

JOHN 4:7-14

Whoever drinks the water I give them will never thirst. Indeed, the water I give them will become in them a spring of water welling up to eternal life.

JOHN 4:14

In Michigan's Upper Peninsula is a pretty cool natural wonder—a pool about forty feet deep and two hundred feet across, which Native Americans called "Kitch-iti-kipi," or "big cold water." Today it's called Big Spring. Underground springs push more than ten thousand gallons of water a minute through the rocks below

and up to the surface. The water maintains a temperature of forty-five degrees Fahrenheit. Even in the brutally cold winters of the Upper Peninsula, the pool never freezes. Tourists can enjoy viewing the waters of Big Spring during any season of the year.

When Jesus talked with a woman at Jacob's well, He mentioned another source of water that would always satisfy. He said, "Whoever drinks the water I give them will never thirst. Indeed, the water I give them will become in them a spring of water welling up to eternal life" (John 4:14). He was talking about salvation.

The refreshment that Jesus offers is far better than any natural spring. He alone, the Water of Life, can quench our thirst. Praise God, for Jesus is the source that never runs dry.

JUST YOU AND GOD

"Lord, it helps me to think of you as like an ice-cold lemonade on a hot summer day. That's how good your love feels to me. Thanks."

45

"THE GUY WHO RAN THE WRONG WAY"

COLOSSIANS 1:9-14

In [Jesus] we have redemption, the forgiveness of sins.

COLOSSIANS 1:14

It was New Year's Day 1929. The University of California at Berkeley was playing Georgia Tech in college football's Rose Bowl. Roy Riegels, a California defender, recovered a Georgia Tech fumble, turned, and scampered sixty-five yards in the wrong direction! One of Roy's teammates tackled him just before he reached the wrong goal line. On the next play, Georgia Tech scored and went on to win.

From that day on, Riegels was saddled with the nickname "Wrong-way Riegels." For years, whenever he was introduced, people would exclaim, "I know who you are! You're the guy who ran the wrong way in the Rose Bowl!"

The stuff we do wrong isn't known by the whole world, but we've all gone the wrong way, haven't we? And sometimes it bothers us when we think about the stupid things we've done. If only we could forget that we lied to our parents—or whatever it was!

Good news! When we confess our sins and repent before God, He forgives our past and puts it away. In Christ, "we have redemption, the forgiveness of sins"—*all* our sins (Colossians 1:14; 2:13).

Don't go around kicking yourself about some dumb thing you've done. Ask for Jesus to forgive you—and then keep moving forward. The right way.

JUST YOU AND GOD

"Jesus, it feels good to be forgiven.
Thank you for saving me!"

Go to the ant, you sluggard; consider its ways and be wise!

PROVERBS 6:6

46
ANT SAFARI

PROVERBS 6:6-11

In his book *Adventures Among Ants: A Global Safari with a Cast of Trillions*, Mark Moffett reflects on his early childhood interest with ants—an interest that never stopped. Moffett earned a doctorate at Harvard in biology and then traveled worldwide as an expert on the subject. His study has given him some interesting info about these busy little creatures.

Long before Moffett discovered the wonders of the ant world, the Scriptures remarked on the skill and work ethic of these tiny insects. Ants are held up by wise King Solomon as a good example for those who tend to be lazy: "Go to the ant, you sluggard; consider its ways and be wise! It has no commander, no overseer or ruler, yet it stores its provisions in summer and gathers its food at harvest" (Proverbs 6:6–8).

The wonders of God's creation are amazing, and God uses His creatures to teach us. God built spiritual lessons into nature itself, and we can learn from creatures even as tiny as an ant.

FUN FACT

Ants do not have ears. Instead of hearing things, they get by through feeling vibrations with special sensors on their feet. Also, their antennae and tiny body hairs can help them navigate without hearing anything.

JUST YOU AND GOD

"I wonder, Lord, can I learn from my dog? I think I can learn patience and true love from the way it treats me."

47

WE'RE SAFE

1 PETER 1:3-5

Praise be to the God and Father of our Lord Jesus Christ! In his great mercy he has given us . . . an inheritance that can never perish, spoil or fade. This inheritance is kept in heaven for you.

1 PETER 1:3-4

ou've heard of Fort Knox, Kentucky, right?

There's a well-protected building there that stores 5,000 tons of gold bullion and other precious items. But it's not like Costco; they are not giving out free samples!

Fort Knox is one of the safest places on Earth. The building has a twenty-two-ton door and many layers of physical security: including unmarked Black Hawk helicopters.

There's another place that's safer, and it's filled with something more precious than gold: Heaven holds your gift of eternal life. Peter encouraged believers in Christ to praise God because we have "a living hope"–a confident expectation that grows and gains strength the more we learn about Jesus (1 Peter 1:3).

Our hope is based on the fact that Jesus was raised from the dead on what we call Easter. His gift of eternal life will always be there for us. God has been keeping it safe and will continue to do so forever. No matter what problems you run into, remember this: If you have trusted Jesus as Savior, you're safe forever.

Even safer than the gold at Fort Knox, our salvation is protected by God, and you are secure.

JUST YOU AND GOD

"Thanks, Jesus, for keeping me safe through salvation."

FUN FACT

When crews built Fort Knox, they used 4,200 cubic yards of concrete and 16,000 cubic feet of granite.

48

A&M'S TWELFTH MAN

HEBREWS 11:32-12:3

*We have many people
of faith around us.*

HEBREWS 12:1 ICB

A large sign at the Texas A&M University football stadium says, "HOME OF THE 12TH MAN." As you know, a football team is allowed eleven players on the field. But at A&M, the "12th Man" stands for the thousands of students who remain standing the entire game to cheer their Aggies on. The tradition began one hundred years ago when the football coach called a student from the stands to suit up and be ready to replace an injured player. Although he never entered the game, his eagerness to help greatly encouraged the team.

Hebrews 11 describes heroes of the faith in the past who faced great trials and remained loyal to God. And Hebrews 12:1 says, "We have many people of faith around us."

You are not alone as you try to live for Jesus. The people who have been faithful to the Lord in the past can encourage you by their example. It could be someone from the Bible or maybe even a grandpa or grandma who loved Jesus. Or maybe it is a teacher, parent or friend who lives for God. They are like a spiritual 12th Man standing with you to encourage you every day to keep going!

JUST YOU AND GOD

"Jesus, thank you for _____. I know I can always count on him/her to encourage me when I'm a little down."

49

THE WONDER OF NATURE

JOB 36:26-33

My ears had heard of you but now my eyes have seen you.

JOB 42:5

A visitor to the California coast who had grown up around the woods and waters of Michigan had some exciting new adventures to see. He found himself staring in breathtaking wonder at snorting elephant seals, barking sea lions, and a forest of silent redwoods. He watched pelicans soar in formation, and he saw migrating whales spouting in the distance. Together these are just a sample of the millions of species that make up the delicate balance of nature.

According to the Bible, the variety of nature is designed to do far more than inspire wonder in our hearts. The mysteries of nature can help us come to terms with a God who also allows pain and suffering.

We see this in the story of Job—a godly man who lost everything.

Here is what we learn: A Creator who is wise and powerful enough to design the natural wonders of our world is great enough to be trusted when we are hurting. Job said, "I know that you can do all things" (42:2). We can trust that kind of God—even if things aren't going our way.

FUN FACT

Two pinnipeds, the sea lion and the seal, have some differences. The sea lion walks on his large front flippers; the seal scoots along on his belly. The sea lion has visible ears; the seal doesn't. Sea lions make more noise than seals.

JUST YOU AND GOD

"Dear heavenly Father, you made the world. I know you can do anything, even help with the really hard stuff in my life."

Woe to you, teachers of the law and Pharisees, you hypocrites!

MATTHEW 23:13

50

THE OTHER BILL HENRY

ACTS 5:1-11

On June 28, 1969, Bill Henry was released by the Houston Astros, ending a seventeen-year major league career. Henry wasn't surprised by the news that the Astros were letting him go at age forty-one.

Bill *was* surprised one day in 2007, though, by the news that he had died. A baseball historian called his wife to express his sorrow after reading of his death in Florida. "Bill didn't pass away in Florida," she told the caller from their Texas home. "He's sitting here next to me."

As it turns out, the Bill Henry who died of a heart attack in Florida was not the Bill Henry who racked up ninety saves in the majors.

He only said he was.

The copycat Bill Henry—actually a retired salesman from Michigan—told his wife and stepchildren and anyone who would listen that he was a former major league pitcher, with baseball cards (the real baseball-playing Bill Henry's, of course) to prove it.

That's an extreme example of something we all struggle with—being who we say we are. Jesus had hard words for the hypocrisy of the Pharisees (Matthew 23). Hypocrisy is saying you're one thing but living a different way—like saying you're honest but cheating on tests at school.

Living a lie is not something God takes lightly. Let's be true to our word.

JUST YOU AND GOD

"I don't want to be a liar like the guy in the story. Help me, Jesus, to tell the truth and not be a hypocrite."

51

ON A MISSION

LUKE 19:1-10

The Son of Man came to find lost people and save them.

LUKE 19:10 ICB

Among the heroes of the American war effort of World War II were the Doolittle Raiders. Their airstrikes using B-25 bombers were important as the United States tried to win the war in the Pacific. One of the pilots, Jacob DeShazer, was captured and held in POW camps in Japan under difficult and painful circumstances.

DeShazer later returned to Japan after the war, but not to seek revenge. He had received Jesus as his Savior and had come back to Japanese soil carrying the message of Christ. A former warrior who was once on a campaign of war was now on a campaign to restore a damaged relationship.

DeShazer's mission to Japan mirrors the heart of Jesus, who came to earth on a mission of love. Luke reminds us that when Christ came into the world, it was not merely to be a moral example or a compelling teacher. He came "to seek and to save" the lost (19:10). He showed His love for us by dying on the cross, and His rescue of us was completed when He rose from the tomb.

In Christ we find forgiveness, and that forgiveness changes our life and our eternity—all because Jesus came on a mission of restoration.

FUN FACT

The B-25 bombers could go 272 miles per hour, and they had a range of 1,350 miles. None of the planes returned, because they had to use their entire range just to get to their target. Fifteen of them ran out of fuel and crashed after the mission was complete.

JUST YOU AND GOD

"I can't believe what you went through on the cross. It must have been scary and painful. Thank you for dying for me. You are awesome."

52

MORE THAN A HERO

JOHN 1:1-5, 9-14

The Word [Jesus] became a man and lived among us. We saw his glory—the glory that belongs to the only Son of the Father.

JOHN 1:14 ICB

For a long time, people have loved watching the Star Wars movies. Whether you enjoy them or not, maybe this quote by a writer named Frank Pallotta helps you see why people like them. He said they show us "a new hope and a force of good at a time when the world needs heroes."

That's something people are always looking for. Even in Jesus's day.

At the time of Jesus's birth, the people of Israel were feeling down. They wanted their long-promised Messiah to come. They thought He would be a hero who would deliver them from the terrible Romans.

But Jesus did not come as a political or military hero. Instead, He came as a baby. Maybe that's why many people missed who He was. The apostle John wrote, "He came to the world that was his own. But his own people did not accept him" (John 1:11 ICB).

Jesus is much more than a hero. He is our Savior. He was born to bring God's light into the darkness and to give His life so that everyone who receives Him could be forgiven and freed from the power of sin.

"Some people did accept him. They believed in him. To them he gave the right to become children of God" (v. 12 ICB). That's why Jesus is the one true hope we all need—whether you are eight or eighteen.

JUST YOU AND GOD

"God, I'm not sure what it all means to be a 'child of God,' but I think it means I can ask questions like I ask my parents. So, can I ask: 'Why do you love me?'"

53

SHOW ME!

2 TIMOTHY 3:10-17

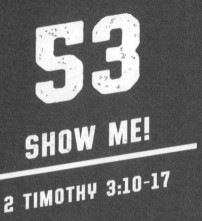

All Scripture is inspired by God and is useful for teaching and for showing people what is wrong in their lives. It is useful for correcting faults and teaching how to live right.

2 TIMOTHY 3:16 ICB

Fixing things isn't easy. Maybe you've watched your mom or dad try to change a headlight or make the toaster work again. Often, they end up finding a YouTube video where someone teaches them with step-by-step details how to get the job done.

Paul was like a YouTube video for his younger friend Timothy, who was learning how to serve Jesus. Of course, Paul had to write an actual letter instead of posting online, but you get the idea. Paul was in Rome in jail when he sent this note to Timothy: "You . . . know all about my teaching, my way of life, my purpose, faith, patience, love, endurance, persecutions, sufferings" (2 Timothy 3:10–11). Paul also said to Timothy, "Continue in what you have learned." He was talking about the stuff Timothy had learned in the Bible (vv. 14–15)—and about how Paul had lived.

Timothy needed Paul to show him how to live by God's Word. That's something we all need to do better.

Who is teaching you to live for Jesus? Find a solid Christian and say to him, "Show me how to be like Jesus."

JUST YOU AND GOD

"God, can you help me find someone who can teach me how to live for you better?"

FUN FACT

There are actually YouTube videos on fixing a toaster. One received more than 115,000 views. There must be a lot of broken toasters out there!

He who guards you never sleeps.

PSALM 121:3 ICB

54

ASLEEP IN THE TOWER

PSALM 121

One of the most dangerous parts of flying an airplane is the landing. As the plane gets closer to land, there is more air traffic, the weather on the ground may be far worse than the weather at thirty thousand feet (more than five miles up), and the runways may not be clear of other planes. Pilots rely on the air-traffic controller to keep track of all the details so every plane can land safely.

Imagine this: The pilot of an airplane full of passengers sends a message to the controller but nobody answers. This really happened. It was later discovered that the air-traffic controller had fallen asleep at his desk. The good news is that the plane landed safely anyway.

Here's even better news: God, our ultimate "traffic controller," never sleeps. We know that from God's heavenly vantage point, our "help comes from the Lord. . . . He will not let you be defeated. He who guards you never sleeps" (Psalm 121:2–3 ICB).

Count on it—God knows what is ahead for you, and He never stops guiding your life. He does this for your good and for His glory (Romans 8:28).

JUST YOU AND GOD

"Since you know everything, Lord, you know what I'm struggling with. Please help me to be strong and do the right thing?"

55

SEEK WISDOM

PROVERBS 1:1-6

The fear of the Lord is the beginning of wisdom.

PSALM 111:10

John Wooden was one of the most respected college basketball coaches in history. As the coach of the UCLA basketball team in the 1960s and 1970s, Wooden won ten NCAA titles.

Columnist Rick Reilly wrote of the coach before he died in 2010: "Of the 180 players who played for him, [he] knows the whereabouts of 172. Of course, it's not hard when most of them call, checking on his health, secretly hoping to hear some of his simple life lessons that they can write on the lunch bags of their kids. . . . Never lie, never cheat, never steal. Earn the right to be proud and confident."

The respect Wooden earned reminds us of something his father gave him when he was twelve years old. It was a list of things to keep in mind each day:

1. Be true to yourself. 2. Help others. 3. Make each day your masterpiece. 4. Drink deeply from good books, especially the Bible. 5. Make friendship a fine art. 6. Build a shelter against a rainy day. 7. Pray for guidance and give thanks for your blessings every day.

Coach Wooden did his best to live this way. As a result, very few people in the history of American sports are as admired as he is.

Like John Wooden, turn "your ear to wisdom and applying your heart to understanding."

JUST YOU AND GOD

"I think it would be cool if someday people could say such nice things about me (like Coach Wooden). Help me live the right way."

56

"FISHING WHERE THEY AIN'T"

LUKE 7:34-48

*When one of the Pharisees invited
Jesus to have dinner with him,
he went to the Pharisee's house
and reclined at the table.*

LUKE 7:36

An old fisherman sits on the tailgate of his truck and looks out over the river for fifteen minutes or so before putting a line in the water, searching for fish. "No use fishing where they ain't," he says.

It was said of Jesus that He was "a friend of tax collectors and sinners" (Luke 7:34). In other words, he hung out not just with people who believed in Him, but those who didn't. We can learn from this:

If we have only Christian friends, we may be fishing for souls "where they ain't."

Being with friends who don't believe in Jesus is the first step in "fishing." Then comes love—caring for our friends by showing kindness to them and saying kind things to them.

This isn't always easy. We need God's help to show Jesus to our friends who don't know Him.

JUST YOU AND GOD

"Here are two friends who don't know you:
_____ and _____. I would love for
them to get saved. Show me what to do."

57

GOD'S FRONT PORCH

PSALM 19:1-4

Praise him, sun and moon; praise him, all you shining stars.

PSALM 148:3

In 1972 NASA astronaut Gene Cernan—the commander of Apollo 17—became the last human to walk on the moon. When asked later what it was like to stand on the moon's surface, Cernan responded, "Looking back to see the Earth in all of its fullness and beauty was like looking out from God's front porch."

We don't have to go to the moon to know there's a Creator. Looking into the vast night sky as he stood on Earth's surface, the psalmist David was convinced. He wrote, "LORD, our Lord, how majestic is your name in all the earth! . . . When I consider your heavens, the work of your fingers, the moon and the stars, which you set in place" (Psalm 8:1, 3).

David wrote that the "heavens" clearly tell of their Creator: "They have no speech, they use no words; no sound is heard from them. Yet their voice goes out into all the earth" (Psalm 19:1-4).

On the next clear night, go outside and look up. Then "listen" to what the stars have to say about the creator God who set them in place.

JUST YOU AND GOD

"Lord, the moon is so amazing! I'd love to go there as an astronaut, but that probably won't happen. So I'll just say thanks for letting me see it at night."

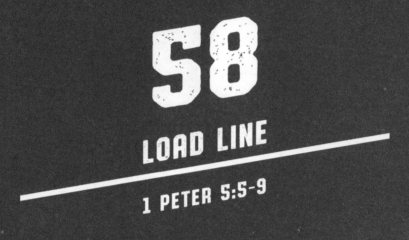

58

LOAD LINE

1 PETER 5:5-9

So be humble under God's powerful hand. Then he will lift you up when the right time comes. Give all your worries to him, because he cares for you.

1 PETER 5:6-7 ICB

In the nineteenth century, ships were often overloaded, resulting in sinkings and loss of life. In 1875, to fix this problem, British politician Samuel Plimsoll pushed for a law to require a line to be painted on the side of a ship to show if the ship was overloaded. That "load line" continues to mark the hulls of ships today.

Even at your age, life at times can feel overloaded. Maybe you have a lot of homework or there might be some family trouble going on. It can make you feel like you are "going under." When that happens, it can help to remember that your heavenly Father can help you carry that load. The apostle Peter said, "Be humble under God's powerful hand. Then he will lift you up when the right time comes. Give all your worries to him, because he cares for you" (1 Peter 5:6–7 ICB).

When life feels heavy, remember that God still loves you very much, and he knows your load limits. Whatever you face, He will help you stay above the load line.

JUST YOU AND GOD

"Here is what is bothering me today: _____.
Can you help me deal with this? Thank you."

God makes people right with himself through their faith in Jesus Christ.

ROMANS 3:22 ICB

59

CRICKET AND CHRISTIANITY

ROMANS 3:21-28

An American visiting Jamaica noticed that the people in that island nation love the game of cricket. So he asked a Jamaican teenager to explain it to him. They sat on the ground, and the teen used rocks and sand drawings to help explain it. Later, the man watched a cricket match on TV while a coach pointed out what was happening. Yet, after eleven days on the island, he still didn't understand cricket.

To be fair, some Jamaicans might feel the same way about American football. One reason we may not like someone else's favorite sport is that we don't get it.

Could that be true of the way some of your friends think about Christianity–that it seems too complicated? Maybe to them, it seems to be about rules and a thick book with big words in it.

However, Christianity is quite simple: Each of us can be made right with a holy God through believing in Jesus–putting our faith in Jesus's death and resurrection to save us. Our sins can be forgiven (see Romans 3:24, 28; 10:9-10). Do your friends not get why you have faith in Jesus? Keep it simple. Tell them Jesus loves them and died to save them from their sins. Maybe they can learn to love Jesus too.

FUN FACT

Cricket was first introduced to Jamaica in 1895 when a team from England played a match on the island. Jamaica was a crown colony of Great Britain at the time, which meant it was not an independent nation as it is now.

JUST YOU AND GOD

"Lord, thank you for saving me. I pray that some of my non-Christian friends can know you too."

60

FLAWED AND FRAIL

1 CORINTHIANS 1:18-31

*God chose the foolish things of
the world to shame the wise.*

1 CORINTHIANS 1:27

Have you ever heard of Davy Crockett? He was an American folk hero who lived between 1786 and 1836. He was known as "King of the Wild Frontier," and he was admired for his courage and leadership.

But he was also very human. Davy Crockett made mistakes and had serious personal problems. This can be both disappointing and reassuring. It is disappointing because he becomes less than a hero, but it can be reassuring if it makes Crockett more like us—just a real person doing his best.

In the Bible we see that God used people who were not perfect. That shouldn't surprise us. God gets the glory if His strength helps us in our weakness. Because He uses weak and foolish things (1 Corinthians 1:27), it means you and I are just the right people to do His work.

The Lord isn't looking for superheroes. He uses regular people like you so His strength and grace can show through. What He wants most is for us to be ready and willing to live for Him.

JUST YOU AND GOD

"My teachers and my parents know I'm not perfect, Lord. I think it's amazing that you love me and want me to do stuff for you. Help me do my best for you."

61

FEEDING THE WOLF

ROMANS 6:15-23

Clothe yourselves with the Lord Jesus Christ. Forget about satisfying your sinful self.

ROMANS 13:14 ICB

An old Cherokee chief was sitting before a flickering fire with his grandson. The boy had broken a tribal taboo (or rule), and his grandpa wanted to help him understand what made him do it. "It's like we have two wolves inside us," said the chief. "One is good, the other is bad. Both demand our obedience."

"Which one wins?" asked the boy.

"The one we feed!" said the chief.

If you are a Christian who is trying to live for Jesus, you understand that struggle. Do you feel that battle in your own heart between doing what is good and doing what you know is not good? The big problem is that if we give in to small, "harmless" desires, we soon give in to bigger sins.

Need help? Trust what the Bible tells us about temptation—we need to run from it. The Holy Spirit can help you. Just ask.

When the chance to do or say something that is sinful comes along, we must say no—over and over and over. Paul said, "Forget about satisfying your sinful self" (Romans 13:14 ICB).

JUST YOU AND GOD

"It's hard to say no, Lord, when all of my friends are saying yes. Can you give me the courage to do the right thing?"

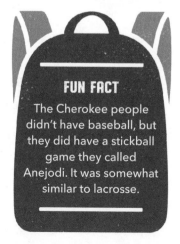

FUN FACT

The Cherokee people didn't have baseball, but they did have a stickball game they called Anejodi. It was somewhat similar to lacrosse.

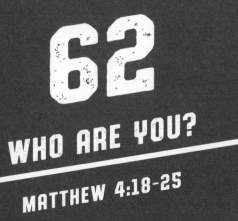

62

WHO ARE YOU?

MATTHEW 4:18-25

"Come, follow me," Jesus said, "and I will send you out to fish for people."

MATTHEW 4:19

If someone were to ask, "Who are you?" my guess is that you would say—"I'm a sixthgrader" or "I play football." But that's not really who you are.

Who you are is based in your relationship to Jesus. If you have trusted Jesus, you are a Christian first of all.

Who you are will control the things you do.

Take the Bible character Matthew, for example. At first, he was a tax collector. In those days, that meant he was greedy and unfair. But everything changed the day Jesus showed up and invited Matthew to follow Him (Matthew 9:9). Suddenly, Matthew had a whole new identity. He became a follower of Christ!

If that's what you are, Jesus wants to make something amazing of your life. And that happens when you try to live the way He asks us to do in the Bible.

Next time someone asks, "Who are you?" answer, "I'm a follower of Jesus!" And live for Him every day. Your friends will notice.

FUN FACT

"Who Am I?" is a fun game to play with your friends. Think of a famous athlete or other person and start giving clues until someone guesses. For instance: "I played basketball for Davidson." "My dad played in the NBA." "I like to shoot threes." Who Am I? Did you guess Steph Curry?

JUST YOU AND GOD

"God, I know I'm just a kid, but I want to be a kid that people respect because I'm a good Christian. Will you help me be that kind of kid?"

For you, who through faith are shielded by God's power.

1 PETER 1:4-5

63

GOT YOU COVERED

1 PETER 1:1-12

Have you ever looked at the gear covering an NHL goalie? The dude between the pipes looks like the Michelin Man with a mean facemask and a logo sewn on his sweater. You wonder how he can move with all that stuff on him.

NHL goalies are padded from head-to-toe. And for good reason! Those pucks are hard!

The walk of faith can be a lot like an NHL goalie battling a power play. Every day, as Christians we face the speedy slap shots of life that can injure our faith. We battle shots of doubt, one-timers of discouragement, and rebounds of temptation.

Like the NHL goalie, we need protection. Just as the goalie needs his pads, gloves, helmet, and facemask, the follower of Christ needs a shield.

The apostle Peter says we have such protection.

Peter writes that through God, believers have "an inheritance that can never perish, spoil or fade. This inheritance is kept in heaven for you, who *through faith are shielded by God's power*" (1 Peter 1:4–5 italics added).

We are shielded by God's power! That can deflect the pucks of everyday life! And not merely in times of trouble. God promises to protect us in every situation until the day Jesus returns.

As a Christian, you are covered—even better than an NHL goalie.

JUST YOU AND GOD

"Thank you for protecting me, Lord. Today can you help me with _____ and _____?"

64

EVERYBODY NEEDS JESUS!

JOHN 14:1-12

Jesus answered, "I am the way and the truth and the life. No one comes to the Father except through me."

JOHN 14:6

A famous Christian was once asked, "Do you believe that Jesus is the only way to heaven? You know how mad that makes people!" In her answer, she said that Jesus didn't leave anyone out: "Jesus died so that anyone could come to Him for salvation."

What a great response! Christianity is not limited to a special group of a few people. It is for everyone—no matter what color or country or anything.

Yes, Jesus did claim in John 14:6 that He is the only way to God. That's because are all guilty before God—we are all helpless sinners. Our sin had to be dealt with. And only Jesus's death on the cross and His resurrection could pay the penalty for our sins. No other religious leader offers what Jesus provides in His victory over sin and death.

This is open to everyone in the world! Nobody is excluded from Jesus's free offer to save us.

Everybody needs Jesus! And everybody can have salvation through faith in what Jesus did for us when He died as our substitute and rose to life to show His power over death.

JUST YOU AND GOD

"I know I do lots of stuff wrong, and you forgive me. Thank you for being my Savior."

65

DISAPPOINTING HEROES

HEBREWS 3:1-6

Think about Jesus. You were all called by God. God sent Jesus to us, and he is the high priest of our faith.

HEBREWS 3:1 ICB

Have you ever heard of Wyatt Earp and Doc Holliday? They were famous gunslingers in America's Wild, Wild West of the 1800s. Through the years, books and Hollywood movies have made them out to be heroes. However, new studies reveal that they may not have been heroes at all.

That's just the opposite of what happens with many Bible heroes. The Bible tells us about flawed people who ended up being used by God for good things.

As biblical heroes go, Moses stands tall. We tend to forget that he was a murderer and a reluctant leader who once directed a rant at God: "What did I do to deserve the burden of all these people?" (Numbers 11:11 NLT).

Not very heroic of Moses! Yet the Bible book of Hebrews says: "Moses was certainly faithful in God's house as a servant. His work was an illustration of the truths God would reveal later" (Hebrews 3:5 NLT). He rescued a whole nation of God's people (in the Exodus).

Real heroes point to the Hero who never disappoints. "Jesus deserves far more glory than Moses" (v. 3 NLT). He's the one who can turn you and me from a sinner into a person God can use for His glory. Isn't that what you want?

JUST YOU AND GOD

"Lord, when I'm playing ball or riding bikes with my friends or building Legos, is there a way to do that for your glory? I hope so. I'm going to try."

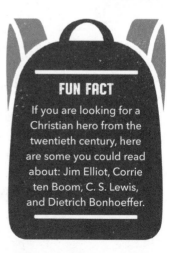

FUN FACT

If you are looking for a Christian hero from the twentieth century, here are some you could read about: Jim Elliot, Corrie ten Boom, C. S. Lewis, and Dietrich Bonhoeffer.

66

WEIGHED DOWN

HEBREWS 12:1-5

So let us run the race that is before us and never give up. We should remove from our lives anything that would get in the way.

HEBREWS 12:1 ICB

August 10, 1628, was a dark day in the history of ships. On that day the royal warship *Vasa* set out on her first voyage from Sweden, but she sank just one mile out to sea. What went wrong? The ship's cargo load was too heavy! The extra weight pulled the *Vasa* to the bottom of the ocean.

Your Christian life can also be weighed down by extra baggage called sin. These are bad things we do that go against God's standards for us.

The writer of the book of Hebrews tried to help us avoid this by saying, "We should remove from our lives anything that would get in the way. And we should remove the sin that so easily catches us. Let us look only to Jesus" (12:1-2 ICB).

Like the *Vasa*, we may look good on the outside. But if on the inside we have a lot of sin, we'll be slowed down in living for Jesus. Rely on the Bible to guide you, and remember that the Holy Spirit can help.

We don't have to be weighed down.

JUST YOU AND GOD

"I don't think I've ever asked the Holy Spirit to live the right way. So that's what I'm doing right now."

If you believe, you will receive whatever you ask for in prayer.

MATTHEW 21:22

67

"YA GOTTA BELIEVE"

MATTHEW 21

At the end of August 1973, the New York Mets were fading fast. They had a record of 60–70 with just thirty-two baseball games left, and most people had given up on them.

Thinking his team needed to do something fast, pitcher Tug McGraw pleaded with his teammates to have some faith. He told them, "Ya gotta believe."

They believed!

The Mets won twenty-two of their last thirty-one games to make the playoffs.

Then they beat the powerful Cincinnati Reds in the National League Championship Series to go to the World Series. Pretty gutsy stuff, huh?

And it all started with a little belief.

In Matthew 21, Jesus tells us what faith can do. He said, "If you believe, you will receive whatever you ask for in prayer" (v. 22). As long as we ask according to God's will, we can trust God's answer.

Jesus doesn't want us to go to Him filled with doubt and lacking the faith that He's powerful enough to meet our needs. All He asks from us is faith.

If faith in each other can help the Mets, imagine what faith in Jesus can do for us.

JUST YOU AND GOD

"Jesus, I believe in you. I have trusted you to save me! Thank you for saving me and forgiving me."

FUN FACT

Tug McGraw, father of singer Tim McGraw, threw the last pitch in the Phillies' 1980 World Series-clinching win.

68

BURIED TREASURE

LEVITICUS 19:9-15

Open my eyes that I may see wonderful things in your law.

PSALM 119:18

Kids who grow up in rural Oklahoma where American outlaw Jesse James (1847-1882) lived are often convinced that old JJ buried some treasure nearby. One group of kids wandered the woods in hopes of digging it up. Often they would run into an elderly man chopping firewood. They watched this mysterious man trudge the highways looking for soda cans—his kind of treasure. Redeeming the cans for cash, he'd retire to his run-down, unpainted shack with a bottle in a brown paper bag. After his death, his family found bundles of money stashed away in his ramshackle home.

This man ignored his own treasure! But we do too sometimes. Did you know there is buried treasure in the book of Leviticus? In seven verses in chapter 19, God teaches us a bunch of stuff: How to help the poor and disabled the right way (vv. 9-10, 14), how to run a business without cheating (vv. 11, 13, 15), and how to respect God in our daily life (v. 12).

Looking for treasure? Dig into the Bible!

JUST YOU AND GOD

"Dear Lord, thank you for writing the Bible. Some of it is really hard to understand, but I'm trying to read it and learn more about how to live."

69

TAKING RISKS

ACTS 15:7-26

So we all agreed to choose some men and send them to you with our dear friends Barnabas and Paul—men who have risked their lives for the name of our Lord Jesus Christ.

ACTS 15:25-26

This may be the best title ever for a book: *Stuntman! My Car-Crashing, Plane-Jumping, Bone-Breaking, Death-Defying Hollywood Life*. It was written by a stuntman named Hal Needham, who has slugged it out in fist fights, raced cars at high speed, walked on wings of airborne planes, and even been set on fire! He risks his life to entertain film audiences.

Now, Paul and Barnabas in the Bible were no stuntmen, but they "risked their lives" (Acts 15:26). They weren't doing it to make movies. Their goal was to exalt Christ through the preaching of the gospel. As a missionary in the Roman Empire, Paul faced shipwrecks, beatings, persecution, and imprisonment—just to name a few (2 Corinthians 11:22–30). But Paul was more than willing to take these risks to tell other people about Jesus.

If Paul could go through all that, what are we willing to do to tell our friends about Jesus? Ask God for the courage to mention to a friend that you love Jesus. Taking the risk will be well worth it.

FUN FACT

Tom Cruise, who does his own stunts, once hung on a rope from the world's tallest building while making a movie.

JUST YOU AND GOD

"This is scary, Lord. I'm afraid to tell my friends about you. Help me have courage and help me think of some good things to say to them?"

70

THINK FAST

2 CORINTHIANS 12:7-10

My grace is enough for you.

2 CORINTHIANS 12:9 ICB

You have to be one tough person to guard the net in pro hockey. A hard rubber puck is headed your way at one hundred miles an hour.

Larry Dyck is a good example. He played in the International Hockey League for several seasons. He was tough and determined. And he was an excellent goalie.

Oh, and he was blind in one eye.

How did Larry handle those laser-like shots at the net? "In hockey, the puck comes so fast you don't have to worry about perception," he explains. This gutsy goalie suited up for both the Minnesota North Stars and the San Jose Sharks in the NHL.

The apostle Paul was another man who did well despite a serious challenge. Paul had a "thorn in my flesh" (2 Corinthians 12:7). While we don't know what it was, we know it was bothersome. He pleaded with God three times to take it away, but He let it stay.

Why? God told him: "My grace is enough for you. When you are weak, then my power is made perfect in you" (2 Corinthians 12:9 ICB).

Sometimes the things we think are wrong with us–too short, can't figure out math, too shy–put us where God wants us to be: depending on His power alone.

So keep your eyes open–and be ready at any time to stop some pucks.

JUST YOU AND GOD

"Can I say thanks to you, Lord, for helping me when things don't go my way? I know you love me."

A new command I give you: Love one another. As I have loved you, so you must love one another.

JOHN 13:34

71

BROTHER TO BROTHER

GENESIS 33:1-11

Brothers like to compete with each other. Whether playing one-on-one basketball or some video game, neither guy wants to lose. It's called "sibling rivalry," and it's not unusual.

That was often the situation in the book of Genesis, which we could call *A Brief History of Sibling Rivalry*. Cain and Abel (Genesis 4); Isaac and Ishmael (21:8–10); Joseph and everyone not named Benjamin (chapter 37). But for brother-to-brother problems, it's hard to beat Jacob and Esau.

Esau's twin brother Jacob had cheated him twice, so he wanted revenge on Jacob (27:41). Decades later, Jacob and Esau would work it all out (chapter 33). But the rivalry continued on in their later families, who became the nations of Edom and Israel. When Israel prepared to enter the Promised Land, Edom refused to help (Numbers 20:14–21).

Happily for us, the Bible shows us that the story of God's redemption can help people who don't get along.

Brothers can become friends. That's the thing with God. When we forgive others, God can change even sibling rivalries into brotherly love.

JUST YOU AND GOD

"God, when my brother (or sister) gets on my nerves, can you help us get along?"

72

ON OUR SIDE

ROMANS 8:31-39

If God is for us, who can be against us?

ROMANS 8:31

A young Christian was working nights at a factory to earn money for college. His coworkers were pretty rough, and he was laughed at for being a Christian. The harassment became more and more vulgar.

One night was worse than the others. The other workers were laughing at him, swearing, and mocking Jesus. He was about ready to quit his job. Then an older man sitting at the back of the room said, "That's enough! Find someone else to pick on." They immediately backed off. Later the older fellow told the young man, "I saw you struggling, and I wanted to let you know I'm on your side."

Maybe you are standing alone against others who don't know Jesus. Maybe on a sports team. Or at school. Look around for a fellow believer to stand with you. But even if you can't find one, you always know that God is on your side. You can never be separated from His love and care (Romans 8:38-39).

Just keep this in mind: "If God is for us, who can be against us?" (v. 31).

FUN FACT

Here are some of the best part-time jobs for high school students: animal shelter worker, babysitter, car wash attendant, grocery store stocker, lawn care worker, dog walker.

JUST YOU AND GOD

"Sometimes, Lord, I think some people are against me. Help me to depend on you and trust that you care for me."

73

THE O-LINE

JEREMIAH 45:1-5

You are looking for great things for yourself. Don't do that.

JEREMIAH 45:5 ICB

When you started playing football, did you tug on your coach's shirt and plead, "Can I be on the offensive line, coach? Please!"

Nope. That rarely happens.

Playing the O-line is the dirtiest, toughest, and least glorious job in football. You only get noticed if you do something wrong: "False start: Number 74! Five-yard penalty."

Seriously. Think about the life of an NFL offensive lineman. They battle men their size and strength—or larger and stronger—whose sole aim is to push them around and crush their "skill" players. If an O-lineman does his job well, he can watch the quarterback or the running back get all the attention.

Offensive linemen work hard but get little attention.

That sounds like some advice the prophet Jeremiah gave to a man named Baruch in Jeremiah 45:5. He told Baruch not to seek personal gain. "Are you looking for great things for yourself? Don't do that!" It's okay to have ambition—but not just for personal gain.

As followers of Jesus Christ, we should be like offensive linemen. We should work as hard as we can to bring honor to someone else—and for us that is our Savior, Jesus Christ.

JUST YOU AND GOD

"Is it okay to ask to be a quarterback? I really want to be one, but if you want me to do something else—or not play football—I'll still trust you, Lord."

FUN FACT

Since 1970, the average weight of an offensive lineman in the NFL has risen 62 pounds.

74

PLOWING STRAIGHT LINES

PHILIPPIANS 3:8-17

Let us look only to Jesus.

HEBREWS 12:2 ICB

Doesn't it sound like fun to drive a tractor? You don't even need a driver's license if you are plowing a field. But as you drop the plow into the soil and head out across the field, you have to pay attention. If you look down at the gauges or glance around to look for birds or wildlife, you'll be in for a big surprise. At the end of the row, you'll look back and instead of seeing a straight line you'll see a row that looks like a slithering snake.

There's a better way. "Plow with your eye on the fence post," is the goal. By focusing on one point across the field, you'll get a straight line.

This is similar to the message of the writer of the book of Hebrews. He said, "Let us look only to Jesus." That way we won't get sidetracked (Hebrews 12:2 ICB).

If we focus on Christ, we will plow a straight path with our lives—not paying attention to bad things—and we'll do just what God wants us to do in life.

JUST YOU AND GOD

"To be honest, Lord, it's hard to stay focused on you. There are so many other interesting things going on. Help!"

Heaven and earth will pass away, but my words will never pass away.

MATTHEW 24:35

75

GOD IS THERE!

PSALM 119:89-96

At the beginning of World War II (1940s), bombs dropped from airplanes damaged much of Warsaw, Poland. However, most of one building stubbornly stood—the Polish headquarters for the British and Foreign Bible Society. Still readable on one surviving wall were these words: "Heaven and earth shall pass away, but my words shall not pass away" (Matthew 24:35 KJV).

Jesus made that statement to encourage His followers (v. 3). But His words also give us courage today. No matter what has happened today at school or at home, we can still trust God's character and His promises.

One psalm writer said: "Lord, your word is everlasting. It continues forever in heaven" (Psalm 119:89 ICB). Psalms also says, "You will be faithful for all time to come" (v. 90 NIRV).

Did you have a tough day today? God is there for you. Choose hope. The Bible reminds us that God's love will never fail.

FUN FACT

More than one hundred million Bibles are printed every year.

JUST YOU AND GOD

"Dear Jesus, I know you see when things are crummy for me. Help me find Bible verses that can let me know you care."

76

GO FISHING!

MATTHEW 4:18-22

"Come, follow me," Jesus said, "and I will send you out to fish for people."

MATTHEW 4:19

Do you like to fish?

There are lots of ways to fish. One is flyfishing. That's when you whip the line back and forth over your head. Then you release the line and set the fly-like lure down on the water's surface. If you are successful, a big rainbow trout will rise, strike the lure, and you'll set the hook. The battle is on!

Halibut fishermen up in Alaska use another method. They go out on the ocean and drop baited hooks 125 to 150 feet into the water. When one of those big, flat fish goes for the bait and is hooked, he begins a long ride to the surface.

Jesus told Peter and Andrew to follow Him, and He would make them "fishers of men" (Matthew 4:18–19 NKJV). As followers of Christ today, we too are to be "fishing" for people in our world. This means we use lots of different ways to tell them the good news of salvation through faith in Jesus.

You're never too young to go fishing. For fish or for people. Do you have any friends who need to hear about Jesus?

JUST YOU AND GOD

"God, I don't really know how to tell my friends about you. Can you help me do that?"

FUN FACT

The biggest halibut ever caught by a fisherman weighed 515 pounds. It was pulled out of the water off the coast of Norway in 2017.

77

MAKE A JOYFUL SHOUT

PSALM 100

Shout for joy to the LORD, all the earth.

PSALM 100:1

Duke University's basketball fans are known as "Cameron Crazies." When Duke plays archrival North Carolina at the Cameron Indoor Arena, the Crazies are given these instructions: "This is the game you've been waiting for. No excuses. Give everything you've got." Clearly, Duke fans take allegiance seriously. They are loud! And crazy!

The writer of Psalm 100 took his loyalty to God seriously, and he wanted others to do the same. "Shout for joy to the LORD," he exclaimed (v. 1). His people were to freely express their praise to Him. They were to focus all their energies on Him and His goodness.

How are we supposed to express our love for God? Lots of ways. One is to pray to Him and tell Him thanks. Another is to listen to songs that praise Him. A third way is to do things for others in Jesus's name—like helping people or being kind to kids others might ignore.

The Crazies are not ashamed of letting everyone know they love their Duke Blue Devils. Don't be ashamed of finding ways to tell God thank you for being so great!

JUST YOU AND GOD

"God, thank you for my parents, for my family, for my church, and for you. I couldn't do this without you."

78

WHERE ARE YOU?

GENESIS 3:1-10

The LORD God called to the man, "Where are you?"

GENESIS 3:9

When two teenage boys heard the sound of their parents' car pull into the driveway, they panicked. How would they explain the mess in their house? Their dad's instructions had been clear that morning as their parents left for the day: no parties, no rowdy friends. But some unruly friends came and the boys let them stay. Now the house was trashed and the boys were afraid. In fear, they hid.

Maybe that was how Adam and Eve felt after they disobeyed God and then heard the sound of Him approaching in the garden of Eden. In fear, they hid. "Where are you?" God called (Genesis 3:9). Adam responded, "I heard you in the garden, and I was afraid because I was naked; so I hid" (v. 10). Sin makes us feel afraid.

Did you know that we can't hide from God? He knows exactly where we are. If we've messed up, the best thing for us to say to Him is this: "God, have mercy on me, a sinner" (Luke 18:13).

JUST YOU AND GOD

"I am right here, Lord, and I admit that I've done things wrong. Please forgive me and help me to live for you each day."

LORD Almighty, blessed is the one who trusts in you.

PSALM 84:12

79

THE FOX AND THE EGG

PSALM 84

Writer David Roper, who lives in Idaho, tells the following story:

"I was sitting by the window, staring out through fir and spruce trees to the mountains beyond, lost in thought. I looked down and saw a fox staring up at me—as still as a stone.

"Days before, I had seen her at the edge of the woods, looking nervously over her shoulder at me. I went to the kitchen for an egg and rolled it toward the place I had last seen her. Each day I put another egg on the lawn, and each day she ventures out of the trees, picks it up, and darts back into the woods.

"Again she had come to my door for an egg, sure I wouldn't hurt her.

"This incident can remind us of something King David said: 'Taste and see that the LORD is good' (Psalm 34:8). How do we start doing that? By reading His Word. As we read and reflect on His love and care for us, we learn that He can be trusted (84:12). We lose our fear of talking to Him in prayer."

The closer we get to God, the more we see that He is good!

JUST YOU AND GOD

"Lord, I try to read the Bible and find out about you, but it's confusing sometimes. I need help figuring it all out. Send help."

80

RISING ABOVE

1 TIMOTHY 6:11-16

Keeping your faith is like running a race. Try as hard as you can to win. Be sure you receive the life that continues forever. You were called to have that life. And you confessed the great truth about Christ in a way that many people heard.

1 TIMOTHY 6:12 ICB

Kris Silbaugh played football with just one hand. What's more, he played *receiver*—a position that's all about using two hands. He even set the all-time receiving yards record at his high school. Born without a left hand due to a birth defect, Silbaugh says, "It has never stopped me. I just don't let it—never have."

New Testament character Timothy didn't let challenges stop him either. He faithfully served God and the church in the city of Ephesus. Paul pointed out two hard things in Timothy's life. First, he was young, and second, he was "sick so often" (see 1 Timothy 4:12; 5:23). It's tough to lead a dynamic and immature church when you're younger than most of the people. And dealing with not feeling good didn't help.

In addition, Timothy had to put up with people teaching the wrong things about Christianity and the sadness of seeing his friend Paul being put in jail and growing old (1 Timothy 4:1-2; 6:5; 2 Timothy 2:3, 9; 4:6, 9).

What looks hard for you today? Just like Timothy did, "Fight the good fight of faith" (1 Timothy 1:18). Ask God for the strength to meet today's challenges.

JUST YOU AND GOD

"You know me God, and you know that life is sometimes hard because of _____. Can you help me overcome that?"

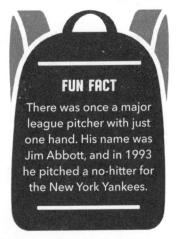

FUN FACT

There was once a major league pitcher with just one hand. His name was Jim Abbott, and in 1993 he pitched a no-hitter for the New York Yankees.

81

WE KNOW WHAT WILL HAPPEN

PSALM 19:1-7

"This is what the LORD says: 'If I had not made my agreement with day and night, and if I had not made the laws for the sky and earth, only then might I turn away from Jacob's descendants.'"

JEREMIAH 33:25-26 ICB

Do you like to plan ahead? Like when your teacher says you have to read a book, do you make a chart to help keep track of how you are doing?

If so, grab a calendar for 2052 (actually, you can print one off the Internet) and circle November 18 of that year. That's the day (or night) when Venus, Jupiter, and the moon will all seem to "gather" in one tiny area of the sky. They will be so close in the night sky that it'll seem like they are one big light. That amazing combo last happened on December 1, 2008.

The fact that we can know when that will happen again proves that God has organized how things work. For instance, there is a comet called Halley's, and we know it will come close to Earth again on July 28, 2061. If there was no set of laws to control the movement of things in the sky, we could not say such things.

Can we see God's hand in all of this? Look at Jeremiah 33:25–26. God uses a scientific fact to prove a point. God suggests that His fixed universal laws, "the laws for the sky and earth," (v. 25 ICB) have the same certainty as His promises to His people.

So mark your calendar, and be amazed by God's unchanging control.

FUN FACT

Halley's Comet swept past earth in 1986. Think about how old you will be when it returns on July 28, 2061.

JUST YOU AND GOD

"Thank you for the amazing things we can see in our world. It's pretty cool that you organized everything so well and gave us just the right place to live in our solar system."

82

PRESS ON

PHILIPPIANS 3:12-21

*I've got my eye on the goal . . .
Jesus. I'm off and running,
and I'm not turning back.*

PHILIPPIANS 3:14 MSG

The Amazing Race has been a popular TV program for many years. In this show, ten couples use trains, planes, buses, cabs, bikes, and their feet to get to the next clue. The goal is for one couple to get to the finish line first.

The prize? A million dollars.

In the Bible, the writer of the book of Philippians—Paul—said the Christian life is like a race, and he said he wasn't at the finish line yet. Here is how Paul explained it: "I've got my eye on the goal . . . Jesus. I'm off and running, and I'm not turning back" (3:14 MSG). Paul did not let his mistakes slow him down. He kept trying to be more and more like Jesus.

We're running this race too. We're off and running! The prize is a lot better than a million dollars. What is it? Enjoying Jesus forever!

FUN FACT

During The Amazing Race, team members cannot be farther than twenty feet from each other.

JUST YOU AND GOD

"What can I do to be more like you, Jesus? Maybe there is a person who imitates you that I can follow. Can you help me find someone like that?"

My sheep listen to my voice; I know them, and they follow me.

JOHN 10:27

83

A SHEEP STORY

JOHN 10:14-30

As some shepherds from the country of Turkey were enjoying breakfast one morning, they were shocked to watch as one of their sheep jumped off a forty-five-foot cliff to its death. But the sheep weren't done. One by one, the rest of the flock—1,500 sheep—followed. The only good news was that the last 1,000 were cushioned in their fall by the growing woolly pile of those that jumped first. Four hundred and fifty sheep died.

Did you know that the Bible refers to people as sheep (Psalm 100:3; Isaiah 53:6; Matthew 9:36)? We like to follow the crowd. Sometimes we do stupid stuff just because someone else is doing it.

But that's not all. The Bible also talks about sheep in a good way. For instance, Jesus himself said, "I am the good shepherd. . . . My sheep listen to my voice; I know them, and they follow me" (John 10:14, 27). It's a good idea to follow Jesus, the shepherd.

What kind of sheep are you? Do you follow other sheep who do dumb things? Or do you listen to the voice and direction of the Good Shepherd—Jesus?

That would be a good question to ask yourself every morning before you start your day. It'll help you avoid a dangerous leap.

JUST YOU AND GOD

"Lord, I'm going to use the question above: Do I follow other sheep who do dumb things? Help me to think for myself, with your help."

FUN FACTS

The world population of sheep is about one billion! By contrast there are around eighteen billion chickens on Earth.

84

THE OVERCOMERS

HEBREWS 11:8-16

Those men were waiting for a better country—a heavenly country. So God is not ashamed to be called their God. For he has prepared a city for them.

HEBREWS 11:16 ICB

How cold was it? It was *so cold* that seven members of the marching band were hospitalized with hypothermia. It was *so cold* that when the referee blew the opening whistle, it stuck to his lips.

It was December 31, 1967, in Green Bay. Game-time temperature for the NFL championship between the Packers and Dallas Cowboys was -13° F, with a wind chill of -48°: It was the Ice Bowl, perhaps the coldest pro football game ever played.

With sixteen seconds left and the Pack out of time-outs, center Kenny Bowman and guard Jerry Kramer bulldozed a crease in the Cowboys' line so quarterback Bart Starr could wedge through for the winning score. A running play had been called because the O-line had done such a lousy job of protecting Starr (eight sacks). In the end, Bowman and Kramer were applauded for their vital role in the final TD.

Like that Green Bay line, Bible heroes usually struggled before coming through. In Hebrews 11, quite a few "losers" are singled out for praise. Abraham lied twice to kings. Jacob was a trickster, thief, and liar (Hebrews 11:8-11). The rest of the list later reveals even more questionable characters, including two murderers—Moses and David (vv. 23-29, 32).

God has great plans for us even though we are not perfect! Nothing can stop us from overcoming for God's glory.

JUST YOU AND GOD

"So, does this mean that when I mess up, you forgive me? I hope so, Lord, because I do a lot of things wrong."

85

HUMAN CHESS

1 JOHN 4:7-12

Dear friends, let us love one another, for love comes from God. Everyone who loves has been born of God and knows God.

1 JOHN 4:7

Do you play chess? Some experts say the best age to start learning to play is as early as six years old. So you may be a bit behind if you haven't started yet.

Here's a chess game that might be just right for you: Human chess.

This was introduced around AD 735 by Charles Martel, who was the duke of Austrasia, which was in northern Europe. Martel would play the game on giant boards with real people.

That leads me to another thought about our friends: Do we sometimes treat them like pieces on a game board? Like if someone kind of irritates you, you don't let him or her sit by you at lunch. You play chess—moving that person away from you. You can probably think of other examples.

God has a better idea. He says we are to see people as created in the image of God (Genesis 1:26). They are objects of God's love (John 3:16), and they deserve our love as well.

The apostle John wrote, "Dear friends, let us love one another, for love comes from God" (1 John 4:7). Because God first loved us, we should love the people He created—not treat them like chess board figures.

JUST YOU AND GOD

"Jesus, I want to love people like you do. Help me to show others kindness and friendship."

86

THE FINGERPRINT OF GOD

EPHESIANS 2:1-10

For we are God's handiwork, created in Christ Jesus to do good works, which God prepared in advance for us to do.

EPHESIANS 2:10

Lygon Stevens loved to climb mountains with her brother Nick. They were experienced climbers and both had reached the top of Alaska's Denali, the highest point in North America. But in January 2008, they were swept off a Colorado mountain by an avalanche, injuring Nick and tragically taking the life of twenty-year-old Lygon.

When Nick later discovered his sister's journal, he was comforted by what it said. She wrote: "I am a work of art, signed by God. But He's not done; in fact, He has just begun. . . . I have on me the fingerprint of God. . . . I have a job to do in this life that no other can do."

Through the memory of her life and her journal she inspires and challenges those she left behind.

Made in God's image (Genesis 1:26), each of us is a "work of art, signed by God." The apostle Paul says, "We are God's handiwork, created in Christ Jesus to do good works, which God prepared in advance for us to do" (Ephesians 2:10).

God made us for a purpose. Can you think of what He wants you to do for Him today at school or when you are with your friends?

FUN FACT

The peak of Denali, which is in south central Alaska, is 20,310 feet above sea level.

JUST YOU AND GOD

"Here I am, Lord. Help me to think of what I can do today to let people know how important you are to me."

87

MAKE IT SIMPLE

MATTHEW 6:25-34

*Therefore do not worry about tomorrow,
for tomorrow will worry about itself.
Each day has enough trouble of its own.*

MATTHEW 6:34

During a radio interview, a basketball superstar was asked about his knack for making game-winning shots in crucial situations. The reporter asked how he was able to be so calm in such pressure-packed moments. The player said he tried to simplify the situation. "You only have to make one shot," he said. One shot. That is making a tough situation simple! Focus only on what is next. Make it simple.

Jesus would agree with that! He said, "Do not worry about tomorrow, for tomorrow will worry about itself" (Matthew 6:34). Worry doesn't do any good; it just makes us feel overwhelmed. It's better to take things as they come—one day at a time—and trust God to help us do the right thing.

As you get older, your life will get complicated. Practice now trusting Jesus and not worrying. Do what's next and trust God with the rest. Make things simple. As Jesus said, "Each day has enough trouble of its own."

JUST YOU AND GOD

"Thank you for this reminder to keep my eyes on today and not to worry about things I can't control."

FUN FACT

Former Los Angeles Lakers star Kobe Bryant set the record for most game-winning baskets in the NBA: twenty-five.

Just as you received Christ Jesus as Lord, continue to live your lives in him.

COLOSSIANS 2:6

88

WHO'S YOUR HERO?

COLOSSIANS 2:6-10

In a survey, 2,000 American eighthgrade students were asked to name famous people they admired and wanted to be like. Those most frequently mentioned were movie celebrities.

Commenting on this, a writer named Sidney J. Harris said he was concerned that each of the famous men and women named was either an entertainer or an athlete. He noted that statesmen, authors, painters, musicians, architects, doctors, and astronauts did not seem important to those students. He said the heroes in our society are people who *have made it big*—but not necessarily people who *have done big things*.

Could the same thing be happening among us as Christians? Do we sometimes idolize the wrong people? James 4:4 says, "You should know that loving the world is the same as hating God. So if a person wants to be a friend of the world, he makes himself God's enemy" (ICB).

Think about this: Do you want to think and talk and act like Jesus? Then think about your heroes. Are you following people who will help you do that?

Following famous people might be okay if we're careful—if they are leading us toward godliness. But the best thing to do is to keep our eyes on Jesus!

FUN FACT

If you are a fan of traditional sports, you might be encouraged to know that there are chapel programs in Major League Baseball, the NBA, the NFL, MLS, and the NHL. Players from many teams meet together at least once a week for prayer and Bible study. That's a good example.

JUST YOU AND GOD

"Lord, I really like to follow these famous people:
_____. *If they are dragging me down, prompt me to find someone better to follow."*

89

MAKE A COMEBACK

1 JOHN 1

If we confess our sins, he will forgive our sins. We can trust God. He does what is right. He will make us clean from all the wrongs we have done.

1 JOHN 1:9 ICB

In the early part of this century, there was a quarterback in the NFL named Chad Pennington. He was an amazing player, but he kept getting hurt. Twice his injuries forced him to go through surgery and tough therapy to get back on the field. But he didn't just play again; he was twice named the NFL's Comeback Player of the Year. Chad Pennington was one determined guy—and he's a Christian!

Sometimes as Christians, we get sidelined. Maybe we did something wrong, and it cut off our relationship with Jesus. We just don't feel good about Jesus because we have hurt our connection to Him.

When that happens, we don't need surgery like Chad did. We need to confess! We need to tell God that we know we messed up. Here's how the Bible puts it: "If we confess our sins, he will forgive our sins. We can trust God. He does what is right. He will make us clean from all the wrongs we have done" (1 John 1:9 ICB).

Jesus gives us hope. We can make a comeback! When we tell Jesus what we did wrong, we know He'll forgive us. That's the greatest comeback of all!

JUST YOU AND GOD

"Lord, today I did a couple of things I shouldn't have. Would you forgive me and help me to do better tomorrow?"

90

GIANTS OF THE DEEP

JOB 41:1-11

God created the large sea animals. He created every living thing that moves in the sea.

GENESIS 1:21 ICB

The blue whale is the largest animal that has ever lived. Some are one hundred feet long and can weigh over 175 tons (by comparison, a Jeep Wrangler weighs two tons). The biggest blue whale ever measured had a heart the size of a Volkswagen Beetle!

In Genesis we are told, "God created the large sea animals. He created every living thing that moves in the sea" (1:21 ICB).

Do you know the story of Job at all? He had lost everything and was very depressed. He couldn't figure out what God was doing. So God did something unusual. He showed Job how great He was as the creator by pointing out some of the amazing things He had created.

He said to Job, "Can you catch Leviathan on a fishhook? . . . There is no hope of defeating him. Just seeing him overwhelms people. . . . Everything under heaven belongs to me" (Job 41:1, 9–11 ICB).

God uses the Leviathan, which many think refers to the whale, and all the giants of the deep to remind us of how awesome our creator is (Romans 1:20). The One who made creatures that cannot be controlled is himself beyond our control and understanding.

The blue whale should make us be in awe of our Creator. All of God's creation points to how great and mighty He is.

JUST YOU AND GOD

"Lord, the blue whale is cool. My favorite animal is the _____. I think it's cool that you made so many different kinds of animals for us to enjoy."

THE BEST FRIEND YOU'LL EVER HAVE

Think about your best friend for a minute. That guy who likes the same video games you like or the same sports you like. You go over to his house, and you can hang out with him for hours. You laugh and goof around and bug his mom for snacks. But mostly you just like doing stuff with him. And you can depend on each other.

How would you like a Friend for life that you can always depend on? And not just a friend for this life, but one who promises you a life of amazing joy and happiness that lasts forever?

His name is Jesus, and here is what He has promised: "I have come that they [those who trust in Jesus] may have life, and have it to the full" (John 10:10).

What does that mean? It means this: If you trust Jesus Christ as Savior, you become a new person inside—a person who is saved from the penalty of all the bad things he does and who is promised a life of peace and joy.

The Bible makes it clear how to have Jesus as not just your friend— but also your Savior! "Believe in the Lord Jesus Christ, and you will be saved" (Acts 16:31).

Jesus Christ was born into this world (that's Christmas), and He lived for thirty-three years as the sinless, perfect Son of God. He was put to death on the cross as a sacrifice to pay for our sins (all those times we did wrong things). Then, three days later, He rose from the dead (that's Easter), to prove His power over death.

What He wants us to do is to put our trust in Him, and when we do, He forgives our sin. We become a follower of Jesus—and that's when we become a new person. "If anyone is in Christ, the new creation has come. The old has gone, the new is here!" (2 Corinthians 5:17).

Speaking of those who believe in him, Jesus said, "I have called you friends" (John 15:15).

That's Jesus. The best Friend you will ever have.

If you don't know Him that way, now would be a great time to put your trust in Him. "For God so loved the world that he gave his one and only Son, that whoever believes in him shall not perish but have eternal life" (John 3:16). Believe in Jesus today!